No Longer Alone

First Church of the Brethren
1340 Forge Road
Carlisle, Pennsylvania 17013

Mental Health & Disabilities Program
Mennonite Central Committee Canada
134 Plaza Drive
Winnipeg, Manitoba
R3T 5K9

phone: 204 261-6381
fax: 204 269-9875

No Longer Alone

MENTAL HEALTH AND THE CHURCH

John Toews with Eleanor Loewen

Foreword by John and Naomi Lederach

HERALD PRESS
Waterloo, Ontario
Scottdale, Pennsylvania

Canadian Cataloguing in Publication Data
Toews, John
No longer alone
Includes bibliographical references.
ISBN 0-8361-9010-6

1. Church work with the mentally ill. 2. Mental health — Religious aspects Christianity.
I. Loewen, Eleanor, 1938- . II. Title.

BV4461.T64 1995   259'.4   C95-930298-0

The paper used in this publication is recycled and meets the minimum requirements of American National Standard for Information Sciences —Permanence of Paper for Printed Library Materials, ANSI Z39.48-1984.

NO LONGER ALONE
Copyright © 1995 by Herald Press, Waterloo, Ontario N2L 6H7
Published simultaneously in the United States by Herald Press,
Scottdale, Pa. 15683. All rights reserved
Library of Congress Catalog Number: 94-73616
International Standard Book Number: 0-8361-9010-6
Printed in the United States of America
Book and cover design by Gwen M. Stamm

05 04 03 02 01 00 99 98 97 96 95 10 9 8 7 6 5 4 3 2 1

*To all the people who have wanted to be accepted as
a regular part of the church and to make their contributions
as best they could under the very trying circumstances
of mental ill health.*

Contents

Foreword

Over the years, as we have had conversations with colleagues and friends, we've often said, "Someone should write a book about this." We were referring to a guide or framework for understanding ourselves and those of us and our families and acquaintances who experience mental ill health. With great expertise and sensitivity, Dr. Toews (assisted by Eleanor Loewen) has written just such a book, full of careful, simple, yet profound truths. The book addresses in a straightforward way such common questions as, Who am I? What do I believe about my relationship with God, about my faith (or lack of it)? How does my faith affect the problems I face?

To encourage us when we were experiencing a particularly difficult time, Aunt Gladys once said, "Life is what happens to you when you have other plans." We are —or see or walk with—those who had other plans but whose lives are broken and difficult for a variety of reasons. As a community of faith, called or to healing in our relationships, we have too often contributed to or perhaps even perpetuated (unknowingly?) the hurt of others, rather than their healing. *No Longer Alone* opens windows and ways to become wiser in our own journeys and as we walk with others.

Even as in Jesus' day people saw "signs" and misinterpreted them, so we can misunderstand and misinterpret signs and symptoms of persons experiencing great stress, depression, and other forms of mental ill health. We are mistaken to think the "process of faithing," as Walter Wangerin *(Measuring the Days,* Zondervan, 1993) calls it, transcends the stuff of life. "What is hidden," Wangerin says, "is the meaning, not the sign itself." Again, Toews clarifies and helps us to understand and interpret what we feel and see and experience.

Toews' wholistic and biblical approach to understanding persons as whole, not as fragments or parts, is an important concept. Other significant learnings have to do with how psychological diagnoses and jargon can be used in unhealthy, diminishing, and disrespectful ways as we tend to label and thus wound people. "Labeling is disabling." It seems when we label a person or behavior, we give ourselves permission to behave and relate in hurtful and even destructive ways toward them.

The flip side is that if we know better what we are observing or can understand what we are experiencing in ourselves or others, we can also begin to relate in healing ways. This may be especially true when certain symptoms or behaviors occur and recur. If we can name symptoms, meaning that we can understand them better, we will not feel frightened, useless, or hopeless—but reassured. This book helps us with that process.

We commend this fine book to those interested, not only in personal growth, but in how we as a community of faith can find better ways to move toward wholeness and health as we relate to others. The questions for discussion are always stimulating and could well be used in small groups or classes.

Dr. Toews shares a story about a man throwing stranded starfish back into the sea. When asked why he bothered (given the millions of starfish he couldn't help), the man answered, "It makes a difference to this one." That illustration effectively summarizes the difference we may make with one person who, because of our commitment to journey with him or her, is *No Longer Alone.*

—John and Naomi Lederach
Belfast, Northern Ireland, 1994

Preface

Books have varying gestation periods. This one has taken at least six years to bring to birth.

Why is it that although mental ill health is more prevalent than diabetes and more widespread than cancer, heart, and lung disease combined, it is hardly mentioned in the church? And why, when prayer requests are solicited, are health problems so predominant—but seldom do we hear people opening up about concerns over mental illness?

The fact is that stigma is strong, even among the people of God. And resource materials for the Christian community are scant.

Hence early in my work as Director of the Mental Health Program for Mennonite Central Committee Canada (MCCC) my advisory committee encouraged the publication of such a book. We worked at several different concepts. Each time I would test these with our American counterparts, the Brethren and Mennonite Mental Health Awareness and Education Committee, who also provided great encouragement for the project.

After a year of discussions, I discovered that John

Allan Toews, a long-time friend, respected psychiatrist, and active church person, had a vision for such a book and was looking for a way to make it a reality. After we invited him to do a workshop on the subject, we were convinced that we had struck upon the right track and the right author. To strengthen the educational direction of the book, we acquired the services of Eleanor Loewen, an adult education specialist. The three of us have enjoyed many hours of working together on the book.

Much work has been done to bring the book into being. One of the earliest projects was to do an analysis of the books currently on the market. Our worst fears were confirmed. There just isn't anything of this kind out there. Then when our field testers sent in their feedback, we heard a unanimous chorus, asking why a book like this had not been written long ago.

Many people have had a hand in this project. The MCCC Mental Health (now Mental Health and Disabilities) Program (MHDP) advisory committee has provided much input. Additionally, the MHDP has provided the funding for the writing of the book. The Brethren and Mennonite Mental Health Awareness and Education Committee has provided invaluable ideas and advice. We sincerely appreciate its sponsorship.

At an early stage we were helped by a reading and consultation group who offered valued critique. Then when we were ready to field test the material, nine people from across Canada and the United States (and representing five Anabaptist denominations) graciously offered to lead groups and to provide appraisal and commentary. Their input was extremely encouraging and helpful, and affirmed the vision we had held.

Recognition must be made of the encouragement offered by many people, especially my colleagues and the board at MCCC. And finally, Annette Schulz, my support staff person, deserves much thanks for her diligent, creative, and painstaking work.

Six years is a long time to work and wait. But I think it was worth it.

—Travis Reimer
Winnipeg, Manitoba

Introduction

"I came that they may have life, and have it abundantly" (John 10:10).

Christ's promise in this verse speaks about health, particularly mental health. Health is more than the absence of disease. Rather, it is a positive state of well-being. However, reaching this goal seems difficult.

Everyone has problems. We don't feel the well-being we think should be ours. At these times we often doubt our faith. When we feel like this we hide from others. We feel like spiritual failures. After all, didn't Christ promise a different outcome?

This difference between the promises and our experience has always confused me. There is the promise of well-being, of wholeness. But when we look around us there is so much evidence of mental illness. The most extensive study on the incidence of mental disorders in North America recently reported that in a person's lifetime there is approximately a 35 percent chance that one will experience a known psychiatric disorder. This does not include the vast number of emotional difficulties that may come out of reactions to the crises of life or from poor interpersonal relationships.

We also know that the incidence of certain conditions continues to rise. Consider depression. The number of people who experience depression is increasing dramatically, and depression is now seen at increasingly younger ages. It used to be rare for an adolescent to be depressed. Now it is commonplace. In the general population few, if any, are exempt from mental health problems at some time in their lives.

We would like to think that it is different for Christians. We reason that surely if the promises in the Bible are true we should be exempt from these troubles. But we know this is not the case. We have problems like anyone else. In fact, as Christians we may feel our problems more intensely because we so often look at them as evidence of spiritual failure and of our not being right with God. So the faith that should help us with difficulties often seems to add to our difficulties.

As I speak on this topic to various groups, one question most often asked is, "Can our view of our faith cause mental health problems for us?" Another way this question is asked is, "How can we have a healthy faith that helps us as we face our problems in life?"

The relationship between our problems and our faith is important in a number of ways. First is the way we understand our problems. In the face of our difficulties, can we draw healing and strength from our faith in God?

Second is the way we respond to persons with mental health problems. We can be agents either of healing or of distress. I believe there is tremendous power for healing in the church, among God's people. However, too often that healing is never realized because we do not know about another person's problems or how to respond to them.

Understanding mental health problems and their interrelationship with our faith should help us become the healing community we are called to be.

This book arose from my own exploration of the relationships between mental health and Christianity as I tried to reconcile what I knew of mental health through the practice of psychiatry with what I experienced in my own Christian life and within the church. I concluded that the Christian faith can be a great force for mental health. I also observed that the way people interpret and live their faith can help cause mental ill health.

These observations led me to propose a Sunday school series on mental health and Christianity for my local church. I did not find appropriate resource material, so I created the content of the series. I then used the material for workshops as well. With each presentation, I became more convinced of the need for people in the church to grapple with mental health issues. Therefore, I felt a book like this might help individuals and small groups explore the interrelationships between faith and mental health.

About this time Travis Reimer, working with the Mental Health and Disabilities Program of the Mennonite Central Committee, became aware of the need for a study book for congregational use. With his encouragement and help, Eleanor Loewen, a specialist in adult Christian education, and I began the creative collaboration of this book.

Eleanor brought her understanding and experience in writing curriculum for adults, adding suggestions and anecdotes, as well as providing the study guides at the end of each chapter.

This Book Is Not . . .

This is not a self-help book guaranteed to produce mental health in fifteen minutes a day. In fact, it is not a self-help book at all, although we hope some points will be helpful.

It is not a book on psychiatry or psychology. In fact, psychiatry and psychology will be dealt with in only the broadest brush strokes. Other resources, such as books, videos, professionals in your community, may be consulted if additional information is needed.

This book does not integrate mental health and Christianity, although many directions for integration are suggested.

This Book Is . . .

What this book *is* primarily about is us as human beings. The book is about the emotions, joys, and struggles we experience as we live our lives. The aim is a resource that provides a framework through which we can view mental health problems, both our own and those of the ones we love.

Because we function in both the mental and the spiritual realms, and because these two realms overlap in our lives, the exploration of the interrelationship of these two areas will be important. The ultimate goal is to suggest ways we can move toward wholeness in our mental health.

No person can be whole in isolation from others, for we were created for relationship. Therefore another goal of the book is to help us explore our own vulnerability or humanness within small groups. This is why questions are included for small-group discussion in fellowship groups or Sunday school classes.

A final goal of the book is to focus on community. In this instance we mean the faith community, the church as an institution, and the informal church where people relate to each other in the name of Christ. This book is a call for us as a community to represent the healing power of Christ to those of us with problems. The point is that in many ways we all have problems and all need healing. We are also called to be agents of healing. This recognition of our dual roles in healing and being healed is an aspect of mental health. So the book is not only about those others who have mental health problems, but also about ourselves and our relationships with others.

Whenever mental health problems are mentioned, people are quick to point out that the emphasis is too much on problems or illnesses and not enough on health. In part this is a valid comment. However, we all have problems. The problems are what create our difficulties. It is our hope that we can connect discussion of mental ill health with discussion of mental health, pointing to ways to move toward health.

We must also discuss confidentiality. In my work as a psychiatrist, I have the privilege of hearing many personal stories. Often they demonstrate beautifully the point I wish to make. Every effort is taken to preserve confidentiality because that is the individual's right and is the basis of the trust relationship I have with them. Therefore, if any examples are used, confidentiality is preserved. In fact, many stories are composites of a number of patients rather than referring to any one patient. However, even as composites, the examples are typical of real-life situations.

The first chapters examine ways in which we can view mental health problems and understand the relationship between these problems and the spiritual realities of our lives.

Later chapters apply the established framework to specific problems, particularly when thinking about applications of the framework. No attempt has been made to be exhaustive, so please see these chapters as examples of ways to view the interrelationships between mental health and our faith.

As noted at the beginning of this introduction, the purpose of Christ is to bring abundant life. May this study be part of that process in your pilgrimage.

How to Use This Book

The book was written with individuals and groups in mind. Individuals might use this for personal study. If it is being used in groups, here are a few suggestions:

It is best that groups give themselves sufficient time to cover a chapter as meets the needs of the group. This means that a chapter may take several sessions, especially if it is being used in a Sunday school class. Additional resources are listed at the end of each chapter. We encourage you to use local community and church resources to supplement the ones mentioned here—for example, public libraries, universities, professional associations, self-help organizations, denominational resource centers.

Be creative. Allow God's Spirit to minister to you as you struggle with the issues presented here and the issues that will come out of your discussions.

—John Toews
Calgary, Alberta

NO LONGER ALONE

1

What Is Mental Health?

Scripture
Matthew 22:37-38

Story

Years ago our family had a topic for discussion at the family cottage each summer. One year it was the saying, "Life is hard and then you die." A number argued that life is not hard. Look at all the luxuries we have. Where there is oppression and starvation life is hard—but not for us.

I argued differently. I claimed that life *is* hard. We have so many challenges, so many threats to our security. We experience losses, fights, and difficulties with our relationships. We have trouble with our moods. We worry and are often immobilized by anxiety and dread. We are hurt. Life certainly is hard for many of us, at least in terms of our emotions. Of course this is only one half of the picture. On the other hand life is glorious, full of joy, hope, good times, and wonderful relationships.

How we respond to all these ups and downs of life is, in part, the realm of mental health. Our basic expectations about life may mean the difference between having or not having mental health.

Focus

When we think of mental health we often would like to equate it with a worry-free, happy life. We may want to add that it should be life with little to threaten or upset us. We are often like Lucy in the Peanuts comic strip, who angrily insists that her life should go up and up and never have a down.

However, mental health is not like this. It has more to do with the way we encounter and deal with the stresses of life. Scott Peck begins his book, *The Road Less Traveled*, with the understanding that life is hard and it is only when we accept this as a fact, rather than moaning about it as if we expect life to be easy, that we start to deal with our problems.

In my work as a psychiatrist I am always impressed that many of my patients seem genuinely surprised that they experience pain, such as through a marriage that has problems or children who don't obey. They protest that life shouldn't be this way. In fact, they often protest when I suggest that they accept life as hard and deal with their problems.

I'm not just being hard on my patients. I notice the same tendency in myself. Sometimes I expect life to be easy. But I soon discover that life is just not as easy as I would like and I had better roll up my sleeves and deal with life as it is.

So, if the easy experience of a stress-free life is not mental health, and if we experience conflict, loss, anxiety, and pain whether mentally healthy or not, we had better look for a different definition of what it means to be mentally healthy.

What Is Mental Health?

Mental health is difficult to define. We know it is a positive state. It is not merely absence of mental illness. Mental health is made up of personal qualities like resilience, adaptability, the ability to tolerate difficulties and face the challenges of life.

The simplest definition of mental health was given by Sigmund Freud, who at the turn of the century popularized psychotherapy for certain emotional difficulties. He termed mental health "the ability to love and work."

Other definitions have become much more complicated. A definition recently appeared in a Canadian government publication. It defined mental health as "that capacity of the individual, the group, and the environment to interact with one another in ways that promote subjective well being, the optimal development and use of mental abilities, the achievement of goals consistent with justice, and the attainment and preservation of conditions of fundamental equality."

Wow! Just what one would expect from a government publication. The simple definition "to love and work" sounds more appealing! What Freud meant was that to be mentally healthy we must be capable of meaningful activity that sustains us (work) and we must be in loving relationships with others. Of course mental health is more complicated than this, but Freud's definition is a good start.

Consider the qualities listed in Galatians 5:22-23—joy, peace, patience, kindness, goodness, faithfulness, gentleness, self-control. How do these fit into the picture of a mentally healthy person? To possess all of these characteristics, all or even most of the time, may sound like "pie in the sky." However, the Bible suggests that these qualities come about through the work of the Holy Spirit. Therefore, an important question that will underlie much of this book (and that you may wish to return to throughout these studies) is whether being a Christian—and allowing the Holy Spirit to work in our lives—will lead us to mental health.

If the Holy Spirit does lead us to mental health, why do we still experience so many problems? We must remember that mentally healthy people will have problems and may get mental diseases. But my belief is that health, taken to these situations, will help us find the right way to deal with what we face.

An illustration may help us understand this better. Let us look at two people whom I knew personally, both with the same problem. Each had the same kind of spinal injury that resulted in quadriplegia, the inability to use arms and legs. Commonly, this injury is caused by diving too deeply or by car accidents that break one's neck. One of these people was mentally healthy, the other was not. The first person, a young man, struggled with despair and became bitter. In fact, the medical and nursing staff dreaded caring for him, because they received nothing but abuse and complaints. He wondered if his life was worth living and thought about how he could commit suicide.

The other person, a young woman of the same age, responded differently. She also had feelings of despair and questioned whether her life was worth living. There was a great deal of anger at what had happened and at God. Then slowly she began to accept the injury as reality and started to grow and adapt. Her energies were devoted to becoming as functional as possible. She reestablished friendships and struggled to resume her career. She still did not understand why she was quadriplegic. But she stopped being resentful of those who could function normally and, possibly more importantly, she stopped blaming God.

Search

The Relationship Between Mental Health and Mental Illness

There are two concepts we must consider. Mental *illness*, as used in this book, refers to a mental disease that has defined characteristics and can be diagnosed by a doctor or psychologist.

Mental *ill health*, on the other hand, exists when people have problems with their attitudes and personalities. They do not have a definable mental illness. Instead they lack the qualities of mental health we just discussed. They do not become involved in really living and dealing with stresses and crises as they come. Instead they whine, avoid, lash out, protest, fight, or do any of a myriad of self-destructive things rather than dealing with the problem. They may have major difficulties forming mature, caring relationships with others.

These two concepts, mental illness and mental ill health may overlap, but they are sufficiently different to require separate consideration. So when I refer to mental illness, I mean just that, suffering from a mental condition. When I refer to poor mental health, I refer to not dealing with the problems of life in constructive ways. If we accept these definitions, then it is possible to have at least a good degree of mental health, even if we experience a mental disorder.

When we consider mental illness, we immediately encounter a problem. The mind, which should help sort out these various attitudes, is affected by the disease. In fact, a person with a mental illness doesn't have the same ability for insight into a problem as those who are mentally well. This is especially true for persons with schizophrenia, severe depression, and mania. It may not be possible to see clearly how mental health applies when faced with mental illness. Yet as these conditions improve, even when there are chronic symptoms which do not go away, it is inspiring to see mental health at work in many people as they struggle with the disease.

When thinking about mental health and mental illness it might be helpful to think in terms of a continuum, from healthy to ill.

healthy ill

Let's take depression as an example. Who hasn't heard someone say, "Oh, I'm just a little depressed. I'll get over it." Where would you place that person on the continuum?

Depression stops being a temporary feeling and becomes an illness when it takes on a life of its own and the person no longer brightens when things are going better. At this point another process has taken over. In the disease of depression the brain biochemistry changes. The brain locks into an abnormal state that keeps the disease going until it has run its course, often months to years, or until treated.

At this point the depressed person often requires medication and counseling to overcome the effects of the illness. The individual may not be able to call on the mental resources within. Therefore professional help by psychiatrists, psychologists, and doctors may be necessary. Of equal importance is the support given to families and caregivers, given their burden in supporting the person with mental illness.

The Model of Illness

How, then, do we look at mental health and mental illness? A formula might help to picture this.

Predisposition + Stress————> Disease or Maladaptation
<————

Predisposition can be anything that makes it more likely that one could become maladapted or ill. It might be a person's inherited genetic makeup. We tend to think of genetics as influencing hair color, how we look, and what familial diseases we are likely to develop. However, to a great extent, genes also determine behavioral and emotional traits.

Predisposition also includes what may have happened in our environment prenatally (before being born). Early environment, our parenting, and the extent to which our emotional and physical needs were met when we were children also form part of predisposition. Any series of adverse events—physical, psychological, or social—can make us vulnerable to turning out a certain way that may be maladaptive, or could give us mental or emotional problems.

This might be a good time to reflect on your own family. What do you know about your parents, grandparents, or extended family? If you are adopted, what information do you have about your family of origin? Can you identify family traits? Do any of these increase the predisposition to certain conditions? What difference could this knowledge have in how you live your life?

Stress is the other part of the equation that produces illness. We can't move today without constantly being reminded of stress. In fact, it is almost fashionable to talk about how stressed we are. And many of us want more than anything else just to be not stressed.

Yet much as we long not to be stressed, stress is an inevitable part of our lives. Stress calls forth the best from us as we deal with the problems of life. Stress also can be crushing. So stress can be good or bad. Partly this depends on the *type* of stress. Some stresses are worse than others. It also depends in part on the *amount* of stress. If we have too much stress, particularly if we are not able to adapt to it, it can be harmful. Each person has a weak point. Sometimes we may not even recognize these points. This may be biological, psychological, or social stress. We respond by getting ill. This might be "bad" stress. It is stress, then, that often tips us into ill health.

Faith and Mental Health

Some people have claimed that faith and mental health don't go together. This point was made by Freud (1889) in his book *The Future of an Illusion*. He suggested that a religious belief is a form of a neurosis. The mentally healthy person does not need such a crutch. By implication, all believers in Christ are neurotic.

Needless to say, those beliefs did not win Freud many friends among Christians, who would claim that faith is not a crutch but belief in a Reality—the living God.

This raises an important point. How can we be sure that our faith is not just a cultural belief or a figment of our imagination that has no basis in fact?

Understanding some aspects of faith in God can make a difference in how that faith helps or hinders our mental well-being. First, faith cannot be proven like some scientific fact (Heb. 11:1). Faith is not subject to the rules of scientific exploration and proof, external validation. Faith in a higher Being (God) is something experienced internally by a person. Faith can be affirmed through personal experience. The psalmist suggests this through invitations such as, "O taste and see that the Lord is good (Ps. 34:8)." So the first test is one's personal experience with Christ.

Second, many people who have mental illnesses have delusions about their faith. For example, a person who believed he was Jesus Christ felt this was revealed through his personal faith. Faith is personal, but it must not be private. Beliefs not shared and tested in community are dangerous because there is no way of correcting distortions.

The extreme of this type of individualism can be seen

in the example of persons who followed the beliefs of one person like Jim Jones, whose followers were found dead in Guyana as a result of poisoning. Sharing and submitting oneself (or group) to the community is a difficult concept when individuals and groups are individualistic and do not consider viewpoints outside their comfort zone. When we look at biblical models, we find that beliefs were processed in a group, whether the group was the children of Israel or the early church.

A third aspect to consider when determining what we believe, and why, is to find a community that teaches a consistency between what is taught today with God's working and revelation in the Bible and throughout history. Hebrews describes this as being consistent with "so great a cloud of witnesses" (12:1).

When we accept that faith is personal (internal), must be tested in community, and is based on God's actions throughout history, we can be assured that our faith is more than a cultural belief, current fad, or even a neurosis.

Going back to the comment by Freud, do you agree or disagree that faith is a defense for those who cannot stand the uncertainties or events of life without something to hold onto?

An example may help us think about this question. A psychiatrist was one of the university resources at an orientation session for new residence hall staff. He cautioned staff to be aware of first year students who came from strongly evangelical, conservative backgrounds. He found that these young people often went to a large university campus to get away from their strict religious home or community. Part of their struggle for independence meant getting rid of the religious bonds.

He counseled that many of these students were unable to cope with the pressures of university life and had nothing to support them. This frequently resulted in attempted suicide. His word to the staff was to encourage these students to hold onto the faith of their parents until they had worked through the issues of faith for themselves and again had something to which they could hold.

Sigmund Freud's belief, that someone who is not able to cope with life without a faith in God is neurotic, is largely responsible for the fear many Christians have about consulting mental health professionals. Many persons think that their faith will be destroyed by these professionals.

Secular psychiatrists will usually leave the question of faith alone, because they consider this beyond their professional expertise and do not want to threaten a person's faith. They recognize that this religious faith may be important to the stability of the person.

An example from my own experience might help underscore this point. I have been in psychotherapy on two occasions, each time with weekly sessions that lasted a little over a year. In one of these therapies I felt it important to tell my therapist, a person who was not Christian, all about my faith. I felt it important that he know that part of me. He responded with respect and thoughtful questions. I believe we both left that session with a deeper understanding.

Is Faith a Defense Mechanism?

A defense mechanism is defined as a way we defend ourselves against anxiety. All of us use defense mechanisms. A number of these are healthy, such as humor and creativity. Others are not healthy and get us into difficulties, such as the defense of blaming others for our troubles.

Some psychological mechanisms are conscious, like determining to not think about a troublesome issue today. Tomorrow is soon enough.

Other defense mechanisms are unconscious. They

serve to remove us from our anxieties, often at the expense of dealing with our problems realistically. Ernest Becker (1973) became fascinated with all the things we do to avoid facing the reality of the fact that we will ultimately all die. He noted that some become involved with drugs or sex. Some look to a partner to meet all needs. Some—architects, people who build businesses, authors, maybe even parents—may build monuments to themselves as creative works to live on after them.

Then he noted another group. They project or place their anxieties onto God. "Cast your burden on the Lord, and he will sustain you" (Ps. 55:22a) is one verse persons rely on when in difficult situations. What other verses can you name that help you deal with the anxieties of life and death? In this case faith in God is used as a defense when facing the anxieties of life.

It is interesting that the above argument must have impressed Becker. He became a Christian while writing a book.

Does Faith Guarantee Mental Health?

Having discussed briefly whether our faith is a sign of mental weakness or ill health, let's turn the question around. Does our faith guarantee mental health?

Faith may be essential to mental health. But it does not guarantee mental health. Christians still experience mental and emotional illnesses, just as they get physical illnesses. We are not spared the realities of life. However, faith may help us toward mental health. It does this by providing us a base from which we can view life (Jer. 17:7-8). Faith is built on God's love and acceptance. Grace allows the continued relationship.

A textbook of psychiatry defined unhealthy faith as one which ceases to be God's work in us and becomes our human attempt to please a God who can never be pleased because we are not perfect, never were, and never will be.

This chapter has introduced mental health as the concept that will be used in this book. We now look at life stages and the development of the mentally healthy individual.

For Further Study

1. Go back to the definition of "mental health" in the Focus section. Do you agree with the initial definition? What might you add, change, or delete?

2. Is faith in Christ essential to mental health? If yes, why and in what way? If no, why not?

3. Considering the section on "Faith and Mental Health," look at the total program of your church (worship, education, verbal and nonverbal messages, traditions, rituals). Who is included? Who is excluded? Does your congregation provide an environment that promotes mental health or one that could contribute to mental ill health? That may be a hard question or make people uncomfortable with discussing responses. What does that say about your group, your faith community, or yourself?

4. How could the opening Scripture be a description of a mentally healthy person?

5. Most of us know people who fit into the two illustrations of persons with quadriplegia. What are some of the reasons for people responding differently to similar life experiences?

6. Using the continuum (healthy to ill), when would you say that a person has moved closer to being ill? Who determines if a person is healthy or ill?

7. What is the attitude in your group or faith community toward mental health professionals? What are some myths about these professionals that need changing?

8. For further discussion on secular versus Christian

professional assistance, you might invite a mental health professional for your session. You might also include your pastor or someone on a ministry team as part of a panel to discuss the topic.

9. When could Bible verses be used as ways of avoiding dealing with one's anxieties and problems?

Additional Resources

Becker, Ernest. *Denial of Death.* New York: The Free Press, 1973.

Benner, David G. *Psychotherapy and the Spiritual Quest.* Grand Rapids: Baker, 1988.

Carder, Dave, et al. *Secrets of Your Family Tree: Healing for Adult Children of Dysfunctional Families.* Chicago: Moody Press, 1991.

Freud, Sigmund. *The Future of an Illusion.* New York: Norton, 1989.

Mental Health & Disabilities Program. *Mental Health Study Packet.* Mennonite Central Committee Canada, 1992.

Peck, M. Scott. *The Road Less Traveled.* New York: Simon & Schuster, 1979.

Raber, Ann. *Congregational Wellness Course.* Goshen: Mennonite Mutual Aid, 1987.

Shelly, Judith Allen and John, Sandra D. *Spiritual Dimensions of Mental Health.* Downers Grove: InterVarsity Press, 1983.

Video:
A Place to Come Back To: Mental Illness and the Church (29 minutes). This resource could be used as an introduction to the topic of mental health and the congregation.

2

Mental Health and Life Stages

Scripture
Ecclesiastes 3:1-8, 11; 12:1-7; Matthew 7:24-27

Story (An Aesop Fable)

The reeds had their home by the side of the river and their next-door neighbor was a great oak tree. When the wind blew, the reeds swayed back and forth. But the oak tree stood straight and firm.

"I can't understand why you bend and lean in the wind," said the oak tree. "I can stand straight and still. The wind holds no terrors for me."

"You are big and strong," said the reeds. "We have learned to bow to the storm."

"Stuff and nonsense," said the tree, who refused to speak to them anymore, thinking they were cowards and fools.

But soon a mighty storm came, with thunder and lightening, terrifying everyone except the tree who stood up tall. But the storm was too strong, and the tree was torn up by the roots and thrown into the river.

"If you had bowed to the storm like us," said the reeds, "it would have passed you over and you would still be standing today."

This chapter is about life, its calm times and its storms, our hopes and our basic fears. It is about some of the needs we can expect at the various stages of life socially, spiritually, emotionally, and physically. It is about facing the storms of life as individuals and with the help of a faith community.

Focus

Fear and anxiety are common occurrences in life. Psychologists have shown that people who are anxious about living are often anxious about dying.

Remember that famous soliloquy by Hamlet? He's walking back and forth on the battlements of the castle wondering whether or not to commit suicide. He starts off with "To be or not to be, that is the question." Then he continues,

> To die, to sleep.
> To sleep. Perchance to dream.
> Ay, there's the rub:
> For in that sleep of death what dreams may come,
> Must give the mortal pause. There's the respect
> That makes calamity of long life.

Fear of what he might encounter was what kept Hamlet from suicide. As humans we must often face the fear not only of what death might be like but also what life might be like.

Life may be lived in the opposite way, not succumbing to fear but accepting it as it is with all its challenges, has been called *ego integrity* by Erik Erikson, the psychologist who first described the conflicts and stages of the human life cycle. Ego integrity is a psychological state. It is also a spiritual state.

It is often revealing to take a look at our lives—past, present, and future. I sometimes ask people to draw lines representing their lives and to talk about the events they choose to mark on the line. That may be something you would want to do now. Draw a line that represents your life. Some people find it easy to note high or low periods with an upward or downward slope of the line. Mark where you are at present. Include a "future" as well.

If you are in a group share your line (experiences) with the group or with a group member.

Another way of looking at your life would be to sum up your hopes and fears at each life stage. What about the hopes and fears of the future?

How we face the future is often determined by how we live in the present. I realized this some years ago, when I saw a family for the first time. As I met the family the wife introduced me to her husband with the statement, "This is my husband, and he will be dead by the time he is fifty." When I asked how they knew this, they told me that all the men in his family had died of heart attacks by age fifty. Why would he be different? The family was facing the stress of the ticking clock.

Sometimes our fears control our lives without our being conscious of them as happened with my son Paul.

At age eight, Paul went to visit his grandparents in a town forty miles away. It was the first time he had ever visited them by himself.

We drove to the highway, and the bus stopped to pick him up.

The next night I picked him up at the same spot. He hardly touched the road as he ran across it. He had had such a great time. He started to tell me about everything he had done. He told me how wonderful it had been. He had been to see the "old grandpa," my grandfather.

I asked, "Paul, did the old grandpa recognize you?" It was important to me that Grandpa, who was getting confused, recognize my son.

Paul stopped as if shot. "Why do you ask that, Dad?"

"The old grandpa is getting old and sometimes he gets confused. I just wanted to know if he recognized you."

He remained silent for a moment. Then he said, "The old grandpa does get confused, doesn't he? And Grandpa will get confused, and then you will get confused." Then he stopped. His voice caught as he said, "Dad, the old grandpa is going to die soon, won't he?"

"Yes, Paul," I replied. "When people get very old it is not long before they die."

"Dad, the old grandpa is going to die, and then Grandpa is going to die, and then you're going to die." Paul stopped again. "Dad, after that, *I* am going to die. I don't want to die. I can't lie there and let them throw dirt on me. Dad, I'm afraid." And he burst into tears.

This event opened the opportunity to talk about death, God, and faith. The next evening Paul repeated his question. We were able to agree that he would die some day, but that he had a life to live first and God was going to help him.

Why is it so important to focus on the life cycle and the experiences we all encounter? Possibly the word *empathy* best sums up the answer. It is through realizing that we all pass through life, with the same fears and stresses, that we come to identify closely with each other.

In identifying with each other we form the basis for relationships that will let us help each other. The Bible speaks of this as "bearing one another's burdens" (Gal. 6:2). Sometimes we lose sight of this. We are often so ready to point to God and the good that comes from being dependent on God that we forget to identify with those who hurt. Or we deal with the situation by thinking, *There but for the grace of God go I.*

This attitude still does not help because it separates us from people's hurts by encouraging us to think we are different or "more blessed." Empathy means that we identify with the other through common experiences, fears, stresses, and joys. Then we can say, "There by God's grace we go together."

Through expression of caring like this, congregations can become places of healing. Let's look at common elements all people face in the human life cycle.

Search

Virginia Satir, an expert in families, commented on dealing with change in a family situation. One spouse will say critically to another, "You've changed. You're not the person I married."

Many think a marriage is over because of the change. Satir's suggestion was to look at it another way, "You've changed! This is exciting! I wonder what change I will see in you tomorrow!"

This chapter is about people, growth, and change.

Life Stages

We often think that children and adolescents change but that adults don't change much. Wrong! Change is a fact of life.

Before we look at the stages in the life cycle, we must understand a little about how the stages relate to each other. In effect, each stage is built on the preceding stage. We deal with the tasks in each stage before we can move to the next. However, these stages do not happen in isolation from each other. A model that might be more helpful is a circular pattern, rather than steps. We incorporate, into the present, what we learned in the past. That helps us move to the future.

Another point must be made. While the general timing of stages may be similar for men and women, the content and issues of the stages may differ dramatically. These will not be discussed in great detail, but may be found in Carol Gilligan's (1982) book *In a Different Voice*.

James Fowler has given us insight into the faith journey. He does not deal with the content or specifics of faith but the *process* of belief. This means he does not deal specifically with Christianity, but what he says helps us understand ways of believing that apply to our own beliefs. How we believe is reflected by our age and maturing in faith. (Note: there is a difference between *religion* and *faith*. Everyone has faith in someone or something. But not all people believe in a particular religion, like Christianity.)

In considering the stages of life, we will use the format Erik Erikson suggested. He discusses each stage with its own unique tasks and conflicts. As we progress through each stage, we deal with the tasks confronting children, youth, and adults. The positive aspect of each task and its negative counterpart will be discussed. A brief comment will also be made regarding the influence these psychosocial tasks have on one's concept of God, on one's faith, and implications for being mentally healthy.

For a concise, accessible description of Fowler's stages of faith development, the book by Thomas Droege (1983), *Faith Patterns and Passages*, is recommended.

1. *Infancy (through age one)*. The primary developmental task is to develop trust. The infant depends entirely on the parenting received. If parents provide the basic necessities, food, shelter, clothing, and love the infant learns to trust the primary caregivers.

If the infant's needs are consistently not met, the infant

develops mistrust. This mistrust can carry into relationships with other persons throughout life. The world and people are undependable. There is no meaning in life.

Developmentally, this is where we develop our capacity for faith. The understanding of God is influenced by the infant's relationship with its parents. If God is referred to as a parent and the infant mistrusts the parent(s), that attitude can also carry over into one's view of God. When we learn to trust, we develop the capacity to hope.

2. *The toddler (ages two through four)*. The task in this stage is to develop a sense of autonomy. This is the time children learn what is right and wrong through exploring their world. Through interaction with parents, children learn how to make appropriate choices between acceptable and unacceptable behavior. When children don't get their own way they may be punished.

It is important that parents set limits for children in a positive way, so the children feel good about their accomplishments. If children can be secure in knowing love and admiration, autonomy and a healthy sense of knowing their own abilities will develop.

Doubting their abilities to determine right and wrong can develop into compulsiveness, inflexibility, and over-control later in life.

The child's image of the parental role also affects how the child thinks about God. Does the God I hear about accept me even if I do something wrong? God is like mommy and daddy.

3. *Early childhood (ages four through six)*. In these years the child begins to take initiative. A set of questions asked during this stage is, "Can I act, express initiative, be aggressive, use my muscles within set limits? Must I feel guilty if I overstep? If I am indeed guilty, will I be forgiven?" The child may be made to feel guilty about some of the questions raised at this age, especially psychologists say, about sexuality. What is right and wrong is not determined by parents alone. Children at this age begin to determine this for themselves.

Caregivers who cannot accept children's developing initiative instill a feeling of guilt over misbehavior. At this stage the child can develop a conscience that is too strict and feel excessive guilt which can carry into adulthood.

4. *Elementary school years (ages six through eleven or twelve)*. If children have learned to trust and have some sense of autonomy and initiative, school becomes the place where they learn that "I can do things well." There is a sense of ability to perform, be skillful as one learns new skills. This is the first time children are really compared to others. Children are asked to perform tasks by a teacher. If performed well, the child feels good. But what of children who feel they don't measure up to others?

The danger, if a sense of success is not achieved, is that the child will feel inferior, inadequate. This child, as an adult, can become a workaholic as the only source of meaning in life. Carried into the church, acceptance and "self-worth" will be based more on doing rather than being.

Think about this as you think about your own life and the lives of adults around you.

5. *Adolescence (ages eleven or twelve through eighteen to twenty-one)*. The main task of adolescence is to form an identity, a strong sense of self. It is the time for determining who we are, which may be different from our parents' goals and dreams for us. If this is not achieved, adolescents may become confused about their identity and their roles in life. This is a painful stage for both parents and children.

Questions often asked are these: What does it mean to be a man or woman? Is it safe to be me—or must I be like everyone else? Why should I believe what my parents or church teach? Will I be accepted even if my faith is ex-

pressed differently from my parents or church? Have I
successfully learned my first lessons of trust, autonomy,
initiative, industry? This stage offers a chance to regroup.

Adolescents are now capable of abstract thought. They
thus can think deeply about complex issues, including
faith and what they believe.

Peers and friendship are important to adolescents. Belonging to a particular group means believing what they
believe. This is a comfortable place to be and stay, even for
many adults.

**6. *Young adulthood (ages eighteen through thirty-
five)*.** The needs of the eighteen-year-old are significantly
different from the thirty-five-year-old. Early young adulthood is a time of developing intimate relationships. This
does not mean that marriage is the only option. Carolyn
Holderread Heggen (1993) makes the point that

> Humans do not need genital contact to be fulfilled and con-
> tent. Married or single, however, we all must have love, af-
> fection, tender touch, and intimate communication to live
> creatively and happily. . . . Both married and single people
> need to be in close relationships with females and males as
> we attempt to develop our divinely created nature in the
> image of God. We were created to be in community. Wheth-
> er married or single we must have close contact with the
> opposite sex to develop our full humanity (p. 190).

Young adulthood is a time of moving from dependence on
parent(s), school, and other securities to interdependence
with other adults.

Pressure is often placed on young adults to make lifetime commitments in what should be, ideally, a time of exploration. The only thing that anyone can be sure of is
facing change throughout adult life. There is no longer
such a thing as a lifetime career. And for many marriage is
not considered a lifetime commitment. Stresses in life of-

ten come from a realization that dreams of the ideal spouse, job, church, life are shattered. Mental ill health may be a result of the inability to meet the challenges of changes in life.

Exploring one's faith is often expressed by being "over against" authority figures through questioning matters of faith. At the deepest level, the person may not really doubt as fully as the questioning implies, but this is one way of thinking about personal experiences and beliefs. A young adult may notice that there are contradictions, that one answer does not solve all conflicts.

This questioning often happens during adolescence but deepens during young adulthood, when young people seem to be "over against" everything that family and church taught them. It is a time of testing the religious beliefs of the authority figures. Young people may turn away from the church because they see adults not living what they profess. They are bothered by the "hypocrites" in the church. They may explore expressions of faith in other churches.

Richard Niebuhr, a noted theologian, wrote of our faith going through periods of "shipwreck." By this he meant that the faith that was to sustain us and let us sail on let us down, because we felt there should be an answer to a question or a situation or that a tragedy should not have occurred. At this stage the person going through the shipwreck experience may return to the earlier concept of the God of the authority figures, or struggle to develop a personally owned mature faith.

7. *Middle age (thirty-five through sixty-five)*. Middle adults assume responsible adult roles in the community, church, at work, and in teaching and caring for the next generation. Otherwise they become personally impoverished, self-centered, and stagnant.

During this period one faces the "empty nest," with

children growing up and leaving home. Studies show that this is a major life change, especially for women. Also, this is the time when one faces parents becoming old and possibly ill, which means taking responsibility for their well-being as well as one's own family.

We are also reminded of our own aging as our bodies show the unmistakable signs of slowing down and other signs of aging.

Finally there is the realization that many of the new opportunities in career and family are no longer there. This too is an adjustment.

By the time one has reached middle adulthood Christian faith is seen in a more comprehensive sense. One develops a broader worldview through interaction with persons from different walks of life and different religions. Middle age is the time of bringing beliefs of childhood and youth authority figures and one's own faith struggles together to form one's own faith.

8. *Retirement (early older age: sixty-five through about eighty)*. When retirement comes there are very important changes to be faced. First is use of time. When thinking about retirement, that is often felt to be the best thing—to be free of schedules and responsibilities and able to do whatever one wants. Many people anticipate being free to spend time on a hobby or interest that had to be put aside during the working years. Travel is a special interest for many. Volunteering appeals to those who enjoy service to others.

Retirement can bring changes that are harder to accept. Those who have found identity and meaning in their work or profession may feel an abrupt lack of status. They no longer are in charge or essential and find it hard to live an unstructured life. Issues such as self-esteem, self-worth, and self-concept can become mental health issues.

9. *Old age (roughly from age eighty or eighty-five).* The struggle is to develop a sense of peace in the face of failing health and repeated losses through death of friends, family, and spouses. As we grow old, our identity as a productive member of society continues to fade, whether our contribution was at work, in the family, or church.

We fear that the future will be difficult, with the reality of isolation, disease, and ultimately death. Fear of death may be an indication of the despair we feel at not having lived life as we had once hoped. How we face these fears will, to a great extent, depend on our faith, hope, and family support and can determine our mental health.

The task of caregivers and pastoral care ministers may be to help the person process that part of the life's journey that cannot be accepted. As Erikson put it, older persons must have opportunity to reflect on their life and come to peace with that life. Psalms 23 and 139 give expression to this feeling of peace.

When it comes to faith, some older adults are often seen as the saints or heroes who show generations after them how to love. They may be illustrated by Fowler's sixth stage, which Droege entitles *I Have a Dream*. These persons are rare. They have a global view of what is good for all people everywhere.

It is important that the older person can say, with Paul, "I have fought the good fight." Life is not viewed with regret and the desperate wish to live it over again. Neither is it lived with resentment of the young.

A Question of Faith

What difference does our faith make in how we deal with changes at each stage of life? What difference does belief in God make?

This chapter has barely touched on the effects transition points in the life cycle can have on mental health. But knowing that people go through a fairly predictable life cycle can be freeing and can inform an understanding of many of the mental health issues which will be discussed in this book.

For Further Study

1. *Personal reflection*   Before we can help someone else, we have to find healing for hurts we experienced in the past. Ask yourself, Do I like myself? Am I running away from some hurting experience in my past? If so, what is it and how can I get help to process the hurt and be healed?

2. *Group reflection*   What is our role as pilgrims who walk alongside others? How can we celebrate each others' uniqueness in the church?

3. In what ways does this study shed light on the Scripture passages from Ecclesiastes? Why does the writer of Ecclesiastes ask us to "Remember our creator in the days of our youth"?

4. Think about the scene of the wife who commented that her husband would be dead at fifty. What fears were expressed? Which fears were left unexpressed? What are the dynamics between the different family members? If you are studying this with a group, take time to talk about the fears of the different people.

5. What did you learn about yourself from the time line and the discussion on each stage of development?

6. Using the time line of your life, describe how your concept of God changed during your lifetime. What made those changes come about?

7. Describe shipwreck experiences you may have encountered. What effect did they have on your life and on the lives of those around you? If you are studying this in a group, take some time to share some of these experiences with each other.

8. What have you learned from other cultures, religious groups, and generations? Is this possible in your faith community? If no, why not? If yes, who or what facilitates this?

9. Who are your "heroes of the faith," persons who provide examples of developing a worldview, of a Christianity that respects and challenges all peoples of the world?

Additional Resources

Bibby, Reginald W. and Posterski, Donald C. *Teen Trends: A Nation in Motion*. Toronto: Stoddart Publishing Co., 1992.

Bridges, William. *Transitions: Making Sense of Life's Choices*. Don Mills: Addison-Wesley Publishing Company, 1980.

Droege, Thomas A. *Faith Passages and Patterns*. Philadelphia: Fortress Press, 1983.

Ellul, Jacques. *Reason for Being*. A Meditation on Ecclesiastes. Grand Rapids: William B. Eerdmans Publishing Company, 1990.

Fischer, Kathleen. *Winter Grace: Spirituality for the Later Years*. New York: Paulist Press, 1985.

Gilligan, Carol. *In a Different Voice: Psychological Theory and Women's Development*. Boston: Harvard University Press, 1982.

Heggen, Carolyn Holderread. *Sexual Abuse in Christian Homes and Churches*. Scottdale: Herald Press, 1993.

Kushner, Harold. *Who Needs God*. Toronto: Summit Books, 1989.

Linn, Matthew; Fabricant, Sheila and Linn, Dennis. *Healing the Eight Stages of Life*. New York: Paulist Press, 1988.

Parks, Sharon. *The Critical Years*. San Francisco: Harper, 1986.

3

Who Sinned?

Scripture

John 9:1-12

Opening Thoughts

John 9:1-12 tells the story of the man born blind, whom Jesus healed by asking him to wash in the Pool of Siloam. The disciples asked, "Who sinned, this man or his parents, that he was born blind?"

It is not just the disciples who ask this question. Often we ask it as well when we try to understand what may have happened in our own or a friend's life. For example, in some circles, if a person is hallucinating and has delusional thoughts, a question frequently asked is whether this is the result of demon oppression or possession.

Possibly closer to home for most of us, if a person is depressed or overly anxious, we wonder if this is the result of a spiritual or mental health problem.

We ask questions similar to those of Jesus' day. Who sinned? Who is to blame? The person? The parents? The environment?

Story

Ben was six when he lost his father in a traffic accident. His father had pulled out to pass a car. They slammed into a car coming toward them.

Ben remembers his father screaming, "We're going to be hit!" He remembers seeing his father sitting there after the accident, blood streaming down his face. Ben called his name, but his father didn't answer. Ben remembers the sound of his father's labored breathing. Then the breathing stopped.

As his mother had died a year earlier, he was now shunted from relative to relative and to the occasional foster home. While at times he looked happy, he could never get rid of the memory of the accident. Nightmare followed nightmare. During waking hours he would suddenly remember the sight of his father's bleeding face.

Ben did not have any wholesome role models while growing up. He started to drink heavily at a young age. He now knows he was trying to forget the intrusive images of his father's bleeding face. Soon he was "lifting things" in stores. Then he ran into a group of people who accepted him, he felt. But they led him to break into houses.

Eventually he was caught and sentenced to jail. Still his dominant memory was his father's bleeding face.

Who sinned? Who is to blame? The person? The parents? The environment?

Focus

We often hear the words *psychological, biological, social,* and *spiritual.* What do these words mean to you? How do we decide if a problem is biological, psychological, social, or spiritual?

Often we assign the problems we see or experience to

a category we understand, such as these above. When we can name the problem, we feel we understand it.

But sometimes it is difficult to categorize a particular problem, such as the struggle of a person with cancer. There are physical issues such as pain and possible death, psychological issues like adjusting to the disease, and social issues like the responses of family and friends. There are spiritual issues as well, related to the ultimate meaning of the disease and basic questions of life and death.

There are also times when someone complains of a pain and a friend comments, "Oh, that's just all in her head." What effect do these comments have if used as labels? What do we mean when we say, "That's all in your head"? What do we mean when we say someone has "psychological problems" or is a very "spiritual person"?

Some people might say that discussion of the psychological, biological, and social is not important in the church. After all, the church is concerned about the spiritual. How would you respond to this? What do you learn from Christ's ministry to others? My observation is that in every instance Christ addressed the needs of the people he encountered—with no concern about which sphere of human functioning contained the need.

Search

In this chapter we will try to understand why the four aspects of a person's being must be taken together when considering mental health. We will consider whether it is even valid to consider people as having four separate parts or spheres of functioning.

Like the disciples, we may be inclined to ask, "Who sinned?" or "Whose fault is it?" in relation to mentally ill people. We often hear this question whenever a catastrophe hits a person or groups of people. Some are quick to think that the catastrophe was punishment for sin or that it had to be someone's fault. Naming the cause of an event or placing blame gives an idea for a course of action and may give a feeling of control. In fact, dealing with the situation based on quick assumptions may not be helpful, because one is not viewing the situation in its complexity. It is not just in catastrophes or disasters that we ask this question. Persons with mental illness often ask it as well when they watch others live lives they wish they were themselves free to lead.

Understanding situations and people is not as simple as assigning a category to a problem—in other words, labeling. The psychiatrist George Engel said that all human illness or reactions have to be considered from the bio-psycho-social perspective to be understood. Nothing in our human functioning is ever purely biological, purely psychological, or purely social. Consider diseases like cancer, AIDS, malaria, emphysema. What causes them? Why do they spread? What are the misconceptions connected with those illnesses?

Consider tuberculosis. Sometime during my first year of university, my tuberculin test converted from negative to positive. However, I never got the disease. Why? The change in my reaction to the tuberculin test means that I had been infected by the tuberculosis germ that is the biological cause of the disease.

Tuberculosis develops mainly in conditions of poor diet, crowding, and little sunlight and fresh air. It seems obvious, then, that we could say it is a disease of poverty. Therefore it is correct to say that it is partly a social disease. Since I had a good diet and all the benefits of a good environment I didn't get the disease.

We can think of other diseases, such as syphilis, gonorrhea, and AIDS, which are often transmitted by sexual contact. In these cases we encounter social questions and questions of morality (the spiritual sphere). This illustrates again the connection among the various spheres of being human.

To illustrate the interaction of these various spheres of functioning in a lecture, I role-played by starting a lecture and suddenly lost my train of thought, got agitated, and walked about in front of the class showing my distress. Finally I told them I didn't think I could continue my lecture. I said the university had a policy that if lecturers couldn't continue, they must give the class a full explanation. My explanation was that I hadn't slept that night and couldn't concentrate. My wife and I had had a fight the night before.

By this time I was very agitated. I moaned, "I should never have said what I finally said. I should not have said, 'You're a slob just like your mom.' "

I collapsed in front of the class as they laughed.

Immediately I shifted focus and asked them to explain what was happening to me biologically, psychologically, and socially. They were prepared to say it was purely a social event. Then I pointed out that biologically my adrenaline was surging during the fight. I had a faster heart rate, increased blood pressure, and dilated pupils. Psychologically, I was experiencing agitation and guilt. Socially, in my anger, I had trampled on a relationship with a person I loved.

When we assume that what is happening to people is purely social, we miss their psychological experience. We must remember that the mind is connected to the body. Thus during a psychological experience the body responds as well. All three levels are active at all times.

This may sound complicated. It is. That is why we must be cautious when we read some of the Christian literature on mental health, because it often assumes that we can look at mental health problems purely from the spiritual level, disregarding the physical, psychological, and social levels.

This is a real problem. I heard a minister state that a number of people were in mental hospitals who were not mentally ill but were demon possessed. This has not been my experience when working with persons in mental hospitals, although I am sure that, as is true for many of us, spiritual issues are part of their problems. However, to attribute cases of mental illness too quickly to demon possession seems another way of saying, "Who sinned?" or blaming a force that can be understood in Christian circles.

It is not surprising that we prefer simple answers to complicated problems. However, it is necessary to consider how complex these issues really are, so that we don't oversimplify what people experience and in doing so do more harm than good. Consider the bio-psycho-social spheres as different planes of a cube.

Any point in this cube has a biological, psychological, and social dimension. The weighting of each dimension varies with the location of the point. For example, a hus-

band arguing with his wife is more social, while a broken leg is more physical, although each involves all spheres.

However, we have a problem with this diagram. We have not included the spiritual in the diagram and have already used each of the three dimensions. How could the spiritual aspect be added to this diagram?

While there is an increased interest in the spiritual dimension these days, I am not sure scientists would know where to include it, for the spiritual realm is not the realm of science but is appreciated only through the eyes of faith.

Paul talks about God as the one in whom "we live and move and have our being" (Acts 17:28). We may vary in how we indicate the spiritual realm. I like to think of it as the ground of our being, permeating the biological, psychological, and social spheres. Seeing the spiritual dimension in this way, we can appreciate events like healing, miracles, or even the tremendous significance of one person just helping and understanding another. Therefore, it is not a sphere of functioning like the other spheres. It is the very substance of our lives. So, when I draw the diagram including the spiritual, it looks like this.

One main idea implied in this chapter is that we bring more than our spiritual selves to church. We bring our biological, psychological, and social selves as well. If I'm worried about surgery I'll undergo Monday, chances are that I'll worry or at least think about the surgery during the worship service on Sunday. I'll interpret songs and words in a different light. I may be looking for words of hope, encouragement, or blessing from the Scripture, sermon, and hymns as well as from friends in the congregation. Think of the implications this has for preachers, worship leaders, song leaders.

So when we talk about mental health, we may need a little reminder that being human includes four dimensions instead of three. With this in mind, we will recall a few basics we might have forgotten from Biology 101, Psychology 101, or Sociology 101.

Let's look at each of the planes of the cube in more detail.

Biological
Genetics
When the disciples asked, "Who sinned, he or his parents?" in a sense they were asking a genetic question. When we speak about genetics we are speaking about characteristics we get from our parents.

Consider the following list of conditions. Which conditions have a genetic component? Huntington's chorea, schizophrenia, manic-depression, depression, alcoholism, anxiety disorders, compulsive personalities? If you said that all have a genetic aspect, you are correct.

All of our psychological functioning has at least a degree of genetic influence. For example, genes influence temperament, personality, anxiety, and the tendencies toward a person developing a disease like depression or schizophrenia.

Brain

For the purpose of this chapter we can think of the brain's influence on our emotional and psychological state as coming from two systems—the cortex and the limbic system. The cortex is the part of the brain responsible for memory and thought.

When a person has a disease like Alzheimer's, parts of the cortex are deteriorating and cause problems with memory. The cortex is also responsible for other functions, such as language, perception, and the ability to move muscles.

The limbic system is the feeling brain. It is the part of the brain that gives us our emotions. The cortex tells us what to think about feelings; it gives our emotions meaning. But the limbic system gives us the emotion in the first place. So when I see a car accident, my surprise, fear, and other feelings come from this part of the brain.

Within the axons (nerves) connected to the limbic system are a whole series of chemicals which control feeling. This is important, because in a disease like depression these chemicals are in much lower concentrations in the areas of the limbic system that control mood. In females the hormonal cycles of menstruation and pregnancy may further affect mood.

There is another consideration. Suicide. How do you feel about people who commit suicide? Is it a spiritual problem defined as sin? Is it a social problem brought about by a state of desperate isolation? Is it a psychological problem brought about by a feeling of hopelessness? Or is it a biological problem? Research has shown that the brains of people who commit suicide often have much lower levels of the chemical serotonin in the centers of the brain that control mood. Does this knowledge, that biology is part of the complex problem of suicide, affect how you view suicide?

If persons have a lower level of serotonin, they may become depressed to the point of feeling hopeless. Depression can be treated effectively with medication. Good treatment also requires psychological and often social help. So once again, the three spheres of functioning are involved in effective treatment.

You may wonder whether biology or psychology drives the thought-feeling system. Obviously both do.

Psychological

The psychological realm is the realm of thinking, feeling, and perceiving. This realm is powerful because how we think and feel determines, in part, what happens to us biologically, socially, and spiritually. Let's look at examples.

1. A woman suffering from cancer is determined to live until her daughter's high school graduation one year away. But she is expected to live only six months. She continues to fight, to will herself to live, and she makes it!

Meanwhile, staff at the cancer center find her difficult to deal with. She is aggressive and demanding in her will to live. However, the staff knows that the determination is necessary if she is ever to see her daughter graduate. A month after the graduation, she dies. She has reached her goal. The will to live leaves her. She accepts death.

Here biology is influenced by this woman's determination and hope. Biology is also influenced by her allowing herself to die after the goal has been reached.

2. An effective treatment for some forms of depression is to help a person correct distorted negative thought. With this form of treatment, many get better slowly.

3. Sometimes we pay the psychological consequences of things that happen to us in life. The story of Ben, with which we began this chapter, is an example. Ben's course in life would likely have been much different without the accident.

Incidentally, when experiencing powerful traumatic events such as this, it is now recognized that powerful, permanent memory traces are laid down in the structure of the brain. These memories keep intruding for many years. Once again we see that biology is involved. We also see the powerful social consequences of the traumatic events.

4. Increasingly we have become aware of the damage brought about by sexual and physical abuse. The church is not immune to this.

Mary lived with her parents, Sunday school teachers and strong upstanding members of their community who presented the picture of the ideal family. As soon as the family would get into the car after church, the children were criticized and the abuse would start.

These parents forced their young children to watch movies where sexual acts were not left to the imagination. The children were then paired with the parent of the opposite sex to try the acts they had seen on the screen. These parents used the Bible to justify the sexual abuse and beat the children when they didn't perform as the parent expected.

Years later, when the children were in counseling, they were asked how they felt about God and religion after these experiences in their home. One girl said that while the abuse was happening she would go off, in her mind, into a beautiful meadow with flowers and a stream, where she pictured Jesus holding her and loving her. That was the only place she got love. And that was what got her through the terrible home experiences until she left at age twenty-three.

We are becoming increasingly aware of the psychological, as well as biological, social, and spiritual problems victims of child abuse are carrying around with them. We are also beginning to understand the effects on relationships later in life. Then there is the matter of trusting others. "Who sinned?"

Social

The stories of Ben and the young woman, victims of abuse, point out disturbances in the social sphere of functioning. We live our lives in the social sphere, in relation to others. We do not know who we are without social contact. In fact, infants die in environments where they are not provided with social contact.

Actions in the social sphere can either hurt, as in our stories, or they can heal. Our families can be places of growth and healing or places of hurt.

This is also true for our churches. They can become places of healing for hurting people, or they can be places that perpetuate the hurt in people's lives through judging, gossiping, failing to accept a person, or judging another person.

Let's return to Ben. While in prison, Ben was visited by a couple from a church some miles away. As they repeatedly spent time with Ben, affection grew. They offered their home for a prerelease pass from jail. When time came, they gave Ben a home while he established himself and looked for work. They also invited him to meet people from their church. Ben reports that for the first time he felt accepted, even loved. It stirred dim memories of home, before Mom and Dad had died.

We have not dealt with the spiritual sphere in any detail. The problems and illness we encounter raise the question of evil in human existence and suggest the possibility of a spiritual aspect to illness and healing. This will be discussed in the next chapter.

For Further Study

1. What does it mean when we hear that we are each other's keepers?

2. How does the discussion in this chapter apply to the teaching/learning mission of the church?

3. If you are studying this in a group, use this topic in a panel discussion, with professional people from your congregation or community as resource persons. Some persons you might include are your pastor, a health professional, a hospital chaplain, and someone who has worked in a culture where tribal medical practices are common.

4. How does, or can, the worship service help or hinder healing?

5. What resources in your community can help you understand how the physical, social, biological, and spiritual influence mental illness?

6. Consider the story of Ben. How would you answer the question, Who sinned? Is sin a factor? Why? Why not? Who are the "Bens" in your church?

7. Notice the headlines in your local newspaper or television news during the coming week. What were the headlines? What were the general reactions to the story? In what ways were the incidents motivated purely through psychological, biological, social problems?

8. How do you feel about a person who commits suicide? What do you hear about suicide? How has your attitude toward suicide changed? What helped bring about the change?

9. Think back to the previous chapter. How does the look into life stages and faith stages fit the discussion about the biological, psychological, social, and spiritual environment?

10. Someone has said, "One Christian is no Christian."

Do you agree? Disagree? Why? Why not? Discuss this quote in light of the content of this chapter.

Additional Resources

Brand, Paul and Yancey, Philip. *Fearfully & Wonderfully Made*. Grand Rapids: Zondervan, 1980.

Kushner, Harold. *When All You Ever Wanted Isn't Enough*. New York: Pocket Books, 1986.

_____. *When Bad Things Happen to Good People*. New York: Schocken Books, 1983.

_____. *Who Needs God*. Toronto: Summit Books, 1989.

Mennonite Central Committee (MCC) Domestic Violence Task Force. *The Purple Packet* (spouse abuse); *Broken Boundaries* (child sexual abuse); *Crossing the Boundary* (professional sexual abuse). Akron, Pa.: MCC.

Yancey, Philip. *Disappointment with God*. New York: Harper Paperbacks, 1988.

4

The Need for Healing

Scripture
Mark 2:3-12

Opening Thoughts

In the last chapter we discussed the spheres of human functioning, making the point that the spiritual aspect permeates the biological, psychological, and social spheres.

In this chapter we will continue the discussion on the spiritual aspects of health and illness. We will consider God's attitude toward health and the role of the spiritual in healing. This, to me, is the pivotal chapter in this book.

Story

Some years ago I went through a crisis in my life that taught me a lot about healing. My career as a psychiatrist has always been important to me. I care about my competence and about what people think of me.

I faced two situations, in close succession, in which I felt rejected and exposed to ridicule. I was terrified. As I worried about these situations I began to get depressed, thinking about the worst possible outcomes for my life. In some ways I felt that all I had valued and worked for was lost. I couldn't sleep, my appetite left, I dreaded each new day. I knew I was depressed and required help, so I spoke to a colleague about the situation and the diagnosis of depression was confirmed.

I also spoke to a number of my Christian friends about what was happening to me. One commented that sometimes God leads us through the desert. At those times we need to learn to trust God. I knew I was in the desert. My mouth was so full of sand I could exhale and have a sandstorm around me. But trust? How could I?

My brother-in-law suggested I see his minister, an Anglican clergyman known for his healing ministry. We arranged to have lunch in a restaurant.

The minister looked at me quizzically and said, "I hear things are tough for you." He queried me about it, then asked, "What is your biggest fear?"

I told him I didn't know.

But he continued prodding until at last he said, "Your biggest fear is that someone will discover that you are not as good and as competent as you wish people to believe you are. You are afraid that your reputation is going to go down and you are terrified that this means the end of you professionally."

He was right.

Then he looked at me and said, "When God decides to change someone God does not fool around. God brings in the bulldozers to get rid of the idols and in the process really lets you have it. Wherever there is an idol that stands in the way, God will work to break it down. We just discovered your idol. You love your profession more than God."

Wow! What a confrontation! I reeled with what he had said.

We finished the meal. I wanted to crawl away and lick

my wounds. In the middle of the busy parking lot, with cars moving all around us, my brother-in-law asked the minister, "Can you give us the blessing before you go?" Before I knew what was happening, the minister threw his arms around us. He prayed specifically for me, that I would identify the idols in my life and yield them to God and have peace. I started to feel amazingly better. By evening I knew the depression was over.

A week later my brother-in-law invited me to his church for a Sunday Eucharist service. At the beginning of the communion service, his pastor prayed a prayer of intercession, mentioning a number of people by first name. To my surprise, I heard him praying for me! Suddenly I sensed that Christ, because of his love for me, had used this man to confront me with my sin.

This condition could have become a severe depression. But this pastor had brought me back to oneness with God. I was humbled.

Focus

Some time ago Jane, diagnosed with schizophrenia, came to see me for her regular appointment. I saw she was troubled. She told me that she had been off her medication for the past week because persons in the church she attended told her she did not require the medication. She should trust in God, confess her sins, and all would be well. To take medication was a sign of lack of faith.

In the process of the conversation she asked, "If I killed myself, how would you feel?" I told her I would feel very sad because I had come to appreciate her and care for her.

She was quiet for a bit, then asked, "If I had to come into the hospital, would I have to first try to kill myself before you would take me in?"

I told her that would not be necessary because I trusted

what she told me about her inner state. I then spoke of being concerned about the church's perspective and asked whether she would resume her medication.

As I reinforced that a number of times, she still looked perplexed. She had tested my caring for her but needed more reassurance.

Finally I said to her, "You know, I can understand where the church comes from because I believe in Christ as the people in your church do. Because I believe in Christ, I wish you could trust me as a Christian about the value you can get from medical treatment."

Telling her about my faith relaxed her. She felt she could trust what I had been saying to her.

The topic of sin is crucial to Christians' views of mental or even physical problems. Note the Scripture passage for today. Christ says, "Your sins are forgiven" to the paralytic. Jane's church considered her mental illness sin. They also saw her use of medication as a sign that she was still in sin, not having faith in Christ. In my story, sin was confronted through the process of a minister's healing ministry. Being "right with God" may lift the state of depression; however, that is not always the case.

Search

Is mental illness sin?

Some argue that depression, for example, is characterized by wrong thinking. Wrong thinking is sin. Therefore depression is sin.

We recognize that much happens in our mental life that is wrong. There are the normal feelings of anger, hatred, jealousy, and anxiety, as well as self-loathing or undue pride. The danger comes when these normal feelings become more pronounced, resulting in emotional/mental problems. Some of this will be dealt with in more detail in coming chapters. In this chapter we will focus on the relationship between mental illness and sin and our spiritual state.

The story of the healing that occurs when the men open the tiles on the roof to let the paralytic down in front of Christ sheds some light on the question of whether mental illness is sin. Notice the close relationship between healing and forgiveness of sin. Christ's first response is, "Your sins are forgiven."

This response was in keeping with the Jewish interpretation of the day. Illness was not confined to one sphere of human functioning. Humans were seen wholistically. If persons were physically or mentally ill, they were seen as spiritually ill as well. So it fit the belief structure of the day for Christ to address the man with the statement of the forgiveness of sins.

This miracle brings us to the heart of how we define sin. Sin can be defined both as act and state. When we consider sin as an act, we have no difficulty recognizing that any act that goes against God's will is sin.

However, considering sin as a state is more difficult. Here sin would be defined as living in a world that is not as God intended it to be at creation. Jesus' statement, "Your sins are forgiven," could have included the acts of sin as well as the state of sin. That statement addressed the profound gulf between the ideal in God's creation—and fallen humanity. Christ restored the person's spiritual well-being.

Another question suggests itself. The paralytic had a physical disorder. If we consider mental illness to be similar to physical illness, why are there so many examples of healing physical illness in the Bible but few apparent healings of mental illness?

Let's look at the healing of the epileptic. Epilepsy was considered a spiritual and mental illness in those days (read Luke 9:37-43). We know that epilepsy is caused by a scarring in the brain that affects the flow of electrical impulses. Note that Christ attributes the seizures to demons. Healing the man among the tombs in Luke 8:28-33 may be the clearest example of Christ healing a mental illness.

Several questions come to mind when looking at these two incidents. How should we understand whether these are illnesses or demon possession? Is the Bible talking about what we now know as schizophrenia or epilepsy? Was Christ healing mental and physical illness? Or is the cause of these disorders demon possession which looks like epilepsy or schizophrenia?

Before the time of Christ, the Greeks saw illness as caused by various "bodily humors" being out of balance with each other. On the other hand, Jews tended to see mental illness in spiritual terms. Consequently they viewed mental illnesses as a disorder of the spiritual realm. This belief influenced the wording of the healing stories.

When looking at Christ's healing ministry, we make a mistake when we categorize illnesses as purely spiritual, mental, or physical. We can't categorize because all of these influences are present in all of us at all times. As was mentioned in the last chapter, the spiritual surrounds the physical, biological, and emotional aspects of our being.

Healing Versus Cure

A patient had a difficult life and had been rejected often by those closest to her. She was very discouraged. Being a Christian, she wanted to follow Christ as fully as possible. No matter how we addressed the problem, she just could not break out of her discouragement.

At a certain point, as I was speaking with her about getting better, she looked at me with tears in her eyes and said, "I have been like this so long that I don't even know if

I want to get better. I don't even know if I could live in any different way."

I applaud her honesty. Christ often asked persons, "Do you want to be healed?" Do we want to be healed? Most of us answer "yes," but for many of us there is a great resistance to recovering.

Many of us hold onto old habits or behavior patterns whether or not they affect our relationships or our personal health negatively. We pull our infirmities around us like Linus' blanket in the Peanuts comic strip. We're afraid of changes. Most doctors know the biggest problem is to get patients to comply with what is necessary for treatment. Like the person at the Pool of Bethesda (John 5:1-9), we can come up with all kinds of excuses for not "getting into the pool" at that time.

So let's consider what it means to become whole and why it's so difficult for us.

First, many of us do not know what it means to be healed. Often we instead want to be cured. What is the difference between the two terms?

A number of years ago I saw a woman was greatly upset by a broken relationship. Week after week she bemoaned her fate. There seemed no inroads to be made. One day she looked at me, hands clenched, and said, "Damn it, I want to be cured!"

I thought about this for a minute, then replied, "You know, I don't deal in cure. If that's what you want you're at the wrong place. Are you sure you don't want to be healed?"

I had determined that she wanted to be made to feel better rather than going through the painful process of change that would be necessary for her to be healed.

Why this distinction between the words? The word *cure* comes from the word *curare*, which means "to bring about recovery from disease." Cure is something done *to* the person. Cure often does not depend much on the person's own initiative or effort. There is an intervention by someone else to bring about recovery.

In our society there are massive technological developments dedicated to cure. We like to think that we can intervene and make people better. In a society built on instant gratification, many people also expect that problems will be easily solved with a minimum of suffering. Even the expectations we have of God are sometimes of the "instant help" or "blessing" variety.

Then there is *healing*. It comes from the word *haelen*, the same root word as "holy." Its meaning is "to restore to wholeness." The only way persons can be restored to wholeness is if they participate wholeheartedly in that process.

Often a person can be cured without healing, and often one may see healing without a cure. Consider two examples. One experiences a tragedy and becomes bitter and resentful. Another experiences the same loss and painfully comes to terms with it, accepts it, and moves on.

Joni Erickson's book, *Joni*, in which she tells of her spinal cord injury that left her paralyzed and her adaptation to it, gives a wonderful view of healing despite the fact that cure did not occur. She continues with her physical disabilities.

Healing may be something that happens to one physically. There are some wonderful examples of that. Just as significant is the healing that happens to a person psychologically as one accepts the reality of what must be faced. Most importantly, healing is the spiritual process of being restored to wholeness.

Healing is difficult work. Our job as Christians is to represent the healing power of Christ in this world.

When considering the connection between healing, caring, and faith we must go further than just defining healing. Healing cannot occur without caring deeply for the person in need. However, if we try to care that deeply, depending only on our own resources, we will burn out, withdraw, and ultimately be bitter and cynical. We cannot sustain that level of intense caring. This can become a difficult situation, especially when one knows that the person needing healing avoids communities that can be of most assistance when facing life's problems.

A caregiver's faith may be essential for dealing with the intensity of a situation when a loved one has a mental illness. Sometimes faith healing has been cheapened to mean a quick hand on the forehead and "Presto! you're healed!" Sometimes healing happens; when it does, praise God. But often healing is a slow process.

This does not mean that we should turn our back on cure. Major advances have been made in treating disorders with medication and psychotherapy. Trained therapists are available to help with emotional difficulties or relationship problems.

There are times Christians delay getting help for too long, because they hope prayer and the support of other Christians will solve the problem. I remember a man who prayed while his wife became increasingly disturbed because of a mental illness. The tragedy was that this was the second episode of the illness. He knew, from the previous episode, that medication and support cleared up the problem.

Arguing for a combination of technology and faith in no way detracts from the fact that sometimes God intervenes in our difficulties in a miraculous way. To me the introductory story in this chapter was miraculous. Others would say it was coincidence that I suddenly felt better. Still others would say that a psychological need of mine was addressed and now it could relax. Some might argue that I wasn't depressed at all. However, my faith tells me it was a miracle.

Most of us can think of examples of the miraculous in our lives. My father experienced a series of strokes that left him quite demented. He was at home, being cared for by my mother, and was having a particularly bad day. He was so confused it was almost impossible for Mom to care for him.

The next morning I asked my wife and children to pray for my father and to ask God to relieve the confusion. We prayed as a family. Later that day my mother phoned and told us of a miracle. Dad had awakened that morning as confused as he had been the night before. He then lay down and fell asleep. When he woke up again all the confusion was gone. I asked what time he had lain down to sleep. It was exactly when we were praying for him.

We considered this a miracle because Mom desperately needed the break or she could not have carried on. In time Dad became more confused and eventually was severely demented. But God had given the relief just when it was needed.

I have no proof for this, but I believe the miraculous is much more common than we think. We dismiss it as chance, coincidence, or luck. What a shame! We could feel so much more cared for if we could see the hand of God in these small miracles of our lives.

One of my patients gave me permission to use this story without changing some of the details.

She had been battling a severe depression for some years. When the loneliness and despair were worst, she felt arms around her, holding her. She had just spoken with me about feeling that God was absent, a feeling common in depression. As we wondered about the feeling of being held, we wondered whether that was "feeling" God present with her. She could take it as a sign that she was not alone.

It is important to recognize the role of God and the

role of people in bringing about healing. There are times when one needs to be "carried" by other people. An example is a woman, at the time of her sister's death, who found it difficult to sense God's presence in the situation. A friend told her that the friend would have faith for her while she was going through the grief. These are the people who intercede when faith is weak and offer support when sufferers wonder whether they can go on any longer.

What happens to us when we become ill or face a major difficulty and we get ourselves tied in knots with thinking and worrying about the situation? We become scared and become preoccupied with our illness. Like Peter (Matt. 14:22-33), we take our eyes off Christ. We sink in our worries and misery. This can become a vicious cycle. How do we break out of that cycle? At such times, we may need to hear Christ's question, "Do you want to be healed?"

If this thought pattern is the negative pole of the problem, the positive pole is the focus on the promises of God. We need a support community that helps us focus on the promises of God. One reason we may not experience healing is looking on it as a private thing between us and God. Having a support community can help us shift the thinking that forms our perspective and expectations.

Another dimension of healing is confession. In the free church tradition, confession is not often part of a public service. It is considered something between an individual and God. We may need to rethink this, particularly in light of passages like James 5:16, "Therefore confess your sins to one another, and pray for one another, so that you may be healed. The prayer of the righteous is powerful and effective."

There are times when confession needs to happen between individuals. Confessing one's dark side takes courage. Consider Larry's experience. He was a minister in a small church and, to make ends meet, he had another job. He had been wronged on the job. While experiencing the wrong, he started to feel so much anxiety that he often could not force himself to leave the house.

As he spoke about his work, he gradually came to acknowledge his anger at those who wronged him. Finally he recognized that he had to forgive them even if it wouldn't change the situation. In the process he also saw that he had to be forgiven for his own anger and bitterness.

He went to see the person who had wronged him. This person considered his decisions appropriate. Larry pointed out how angry he felt about the situation, asked for forgiveness, and sought to reestablish the relationship.

Larry's fears faded during the following months. He was amazed that the crippling anxiety had fled. The work situation wasn't changed, but the spirit was healed.

The primary emphasis in this chapter is the role of the individual. What about corporate sins, the sins of the community? Do faith communities also need to respond to Christ's question, "Do you want to be healed?"

Welton Gaddy (1992, p. 127) comments on the role of healing, caring, and faith through public confession in worship. He says,

> Confessing sins is the hardest work of worship. In this act, worshipers have to confront the dark sides of their natures with stark honesty and ponder the consequences of their unforgiven sins realistically. Nobody likes to do that. But all need the experience.
>
> Most people need assistance in making confessions. Culture conditions us to disguise our weaknesses, cover our faults, reject guilt, and remain silent about our sins. Worship demands a dramatic turn around from that—confession at all costs. Not surprisingly, help is needed.

Consider the interrelationship of the spiritual with other spheres of functioning when working through the rest of the book.

For Further Study

1. What is your definition of sin?

2. How would you describe the relationship between sin and spiritual well-being?

3. If someone in your group has been in a country where traditional medicines are practiced, have them share the role of these traditional medicines. How do, or could, contemporary and traditional medical practices co-operate? What would be the advantages and disadvantages?

4. What are your responses to the woman who didn't know if she wanted to get better? How do we minister to persons who fear getting healed/cured?

5. Describe a situation where you have tried to minister to a person who has ostracized him/herself from those who could provide a caring, supportive community. Did the relationship get to the point where you had to realize that there was nothing more you could do for the person and had to discontinue the relationship? What were the dynamics of that decision, particularly as you tried to reconcile the action with the desire to be a caring Christian?

6. Describe a situation where God is tested by avoiding effective medical assistance in finding a cure or healing.

7. Tell each other stories of cures and healing.

8. Study such additional references concerning confession and healing as Leviticus 5:5, Numbers 5:6-7, Psalm 32:5, James 5:16, 1 John 1:9.

9. How might worship services be times of healing and caring? What changes in worship experiences would need to happen in your congregation?

10. Discuss the need and place for confessing group sins.

Additional Resources

Erickson, Joni. *Joni*. Grand Rapids: Zondervan, 1976.

Gaddy, C. Welton. *The Gift of Worship*. Nashville: Broadman Press, 1992.

Malony, H. Newton (ed.). *Wholeness and Holiness: Readings in the Psychology/Theology of Mental Health*. Grand Rapids: Baker, 1983.

Montgomery, John Warwick (ed.). *Demon Possession*. Bethany House, 1976.

Occasional Papers No. 11. *Essays on Spiritual Bondage and Deliverance*. Elkhart: Associated Mennonite Biblical Seminaries, 1989.

Peck, M. Scott. *People of the Lie*. New York: Simon and Schuster, 1983.

Sanford, John A. *Healing and Wholeness*. New York: Paulist, 1977.

Vanier, Jean. (1988). *The Broken Body: Journey to Wholeness*. New York: Paulist, 1988.

Videos:

Is Any Among You Suffering? Firsthand testimonies of Christians (from the Brethren tradition) on the meaning of anointing. Examination of the biblical and covenantal aspects of the anointing service and its use in private and public settings. Seventeen minutes.

5

Emotions That Hurt— Emotions That Heal

Scripture

Mark 11:15-18; Matthew 21:18-21; Ephesians 4:26

Opening Thoughts

In the first number of studies we described how we function as humans. We looked at health and illness and wondered why it is so hard to accept healing. Many of our problems involve our emotions or arise from difficulties with our emotions. This chapter deals with emotional responses to life situations, especially the emotion most difficult to control—anger.

Story

When I first met Ralph he was forty-three. He had been married for six happy years, he thought. You could always count on Ralph when there was a job to be done. Consequently he was always sought after to perform various duties in the church. He was there night after night and all day most Saturdays.

He told me, one day, that his wife, Angela, had announced to him the night before that, if things did not change in their marriage, she would have to leave him. He was dumbfounded. Wasn't the marriage solid? He was faithful to her. He was a good provider. He saw to it that their three children had everything they needed.

Angela acknowledged that he was all these things. What distressed her most was that she did not feel she knew him. He was never there for her. Even when he was at home, he wasn't there. If she wanted to express how she felt about something, Ralph would not understand it. He kept telling her she should not feel that way and should just think about her feelings rationally.

Angela noted that at first she had felt lonely when Ralph became so involved in the church. In time she had begun to resent it. Now she felt she needed a husband and the children needed a father. She added, "Ralph, I know you are a good man, but I don't think we can make it. I need someone who will be with me, who will hear me, and will share feelings with me. But whenever I have feelings, you shut them out and run to church. What's more, I don't know what you feel yourself. All you do is give advice. I need more than that."

Ralph told me the story with no trace of emotion except for some anxious playing with his fingers. He was confused. As we spoke more about this, the following story emerged. As a child, Ralph had been big for his age. If he cried his mother scolded him, "You're too big to cry." When he got angry he was told, "Be careful! If you don't control your anger you may kill someone." Dad left the family when Ralph was eight, and Ralph was told, "Now you have to be strong for mommy."

At age nine Ralph got involved in a fight on the way home from school. He hit his tormentor on the nose and suddenly there was blood everywhere. This scared him, especially when he was again told that his anger could kill if he didn't control it.

So Ralph stopped feeling. He used to tell himself that he didn't feel. If hurt, he would not cry. He learned to think, to rationalize, and to explain. If the situation was tense, he would just leave.

Ralph remembers what attracted him to Angela—she did have emotions. She was full of life and enthusiasm. However, shortly after the marriage Ralph began to find it more comfortable not to be home, because Angela would get angry or cry or fret about things. Ralph felt better in church, where he could discuss problems and plan solutions.

Focus

All of us have emotions. But we differ in the extent to which we feel and express them. Some of us deal with life issues by thinking through the issues (thought) and some deal with these issues with emotional (feeling) responses. Neither is right or wrong, just different.

Some people are well-integrated. They are able to think situations through rationally and can also respond through their feelings. Persons who only respond rationally, analyzing every situation, rarely shed a tear. They seldom express anger and, like Ralph, rarely experience deep emotion of any kind.

Others emote. They experience feelings and express them whether appropriate or not. These people seldom think about their feelings and attempt to understand them. At either of these extremes there is trouble. People controlled by their emotions rarely experience stability in relationships.

On the other hand, people who are purely analytical may or may not be aware that something is missing in their lives. They remain confused by the emotional responses of others. Because they don't recognize or express their feelings, they have difficulty sustaining caring relationships or understanding emotional persons.

An emotionally healthy, mature person is able to integrate thoughts and feelings. To illustrate this, think of a piano piece played technically. It's perfect. Every note is in place with the correct timing. However, technical playing just doesn't sound right. Now add the expression, emotional interpretation, of the pianist who puts herself into the piece. Suddenly the piece comes alive, touching the "head and heart" of the listener.

Search

Emergency Emotions—Welfare Emotions

In his book *Lifesigns*, Henri Nouwen (1989) describes us as living in the house of fear, beset by the anxieties of life. He points out that we were never intended to live in fear. Instead, the Holy Spirit in us is to lead us from the house of fear to the house of love where God lives and wants us to be.

Christ says, "Consider the lilies of the field, how they grow; they neither toil nor spin, yet I tell you, even Solomon in all his glory was not clothed like one of these. . . . So do not worry about tomorrow, for tomorrow will bring worries of its own. Today's trouble is enough for today" (Matt. 6:28-29, 34).

Reaching that state of peace and contentment can be difficult. Our natural response to threatening or unpleasant situations will more likely lead to emotions like anxiety and anger. Some of us are natural worriers. We worry about everything. And when we don't have anything to worry about, we worry about not worrying!

The problem is increased in the presence of emotional

illness such as anxiety disorders or depression. Understanding emotional responses can help us understand ourselves and others better. Maybe we can avoid situations such as Ralph's.

Emotions can be divided roughly into two categories—*emergency* emotions and *welfare* emotions. Emergency emotions prompt us to be ready to defend ourselves against threatening situations. These include anger, rage, fear, anxiety, and guilt. Emergency emotions are our defense mechanisms for dealing with immediate situations and are rarely pleasant.

Then there are the emotions that help us relax and give a feeling of peace and contentment. These are emotions like joy, happiness, love, and hope. They have been called the "welfare emotions." These emotions build up rather than destroy and can prepare us to deal with the next challenge that comes along.

Emergency Emotions

We noted that emergency emotions arise from a threat, real or imagined. What do we mean by "threat"? Usually we recognize a threat—when our safety is challenged either directly or indirectly—by the feeling that something important to us may no longer be available.

Fear may be turned into anxiety, anger, or rage. One emotion can lead to another. Often a person will respond to fear with anger in an attempt to gain control of a situation. Children learn this from an early age. For example, a six-month-old child has a way of letting an older sibling know when personal well-being is threatened. A good squeal will soon get an adult's attention.

Psychologists tell us that we also respond with emergency emotions when a "supply" that we depend on is threatened. That supply may be a physical survival need like food, shelter, and clothing, or emotional need like love. For example, I may have a fight with my wife. After the sound and fury, when we still aren't talking, I feel scared and maybe a bit angry, sad, and confused. Why? I am afraid that a barrier has been placed between my wife and me and that the emotional supply of love I need will be withdrawn.

In my work as a psychiatrist, I see the results in adults of absence of love or overly conditional love when they were children. If love is absent, children may search forever for someone to fill that void in their lives. Until people learn to trust and love again, they may have lifelong difficulty establishing mature, caring relationships. This ties in, again, with the discussion in chapter two.

A person traumatized as a child has a hard time responding to people in adult relationships since there is too much reliance on emergency emotions. Suicide attempts may follow troubles in these relationships, as the person feels hopeless and desperate, particularly if each relationship breaks down.

There are two basic human responses to these situations. Either the person withdraws into isolation and never forms close relationships. Or, in a desperate search for love, the person tries to get too close too soon. Some common examples are persons who marry on the rebound after divorce or the death of a spouse. One person's eagerness for love and affection may smother the other person until one of them withdraws from the relationship or the relationship breaks down.

Sometimes this search for love will take the person into promiscuity or other destructive relationships. Others, however, are able to find, form, and maintain healthy relationships. They are able to surround themselves with people who can be good for them and help them.

Anger

Anger is an emotional state that presents great difficulty for Christians. We are taught that we should not be angry. Ephesians 4:26 is often used as a reminder that we should not get angry when, in fact, it says that we should not sin when angry. Anger is a normal human response to a threat—real or symbolic—to ourselves or our values.

An example of a threat to values is Christ clearing the temple. There was a rage that said, "You can't do this!" The temple was symbolically important to Christ. It was the house of God being desecrated through the activities of the hawkers and money changers. The outrage was too much for Christ to hold his emotions in check, so he expressed his anger by turning over tables and driving out the merchants (Mark 11:15-17).

Many feel anger and express it destructively. They blow up and attack other people verbally or physically. Anger can be triggered by a word, by an action that is not appreciated, sometimes even by a thought. Anger often erupts when we feel we are not in control.

Often children are abused by an angry parent because the children do not do just as the parent wants. Parents feel that they are losing control of children or situations.

The same happens in marriage relationships. Spouse abuse is common, even among members in the Christian church. Any couple will have their difficulties and their disagreements. But if one partner, usually the male, has to be in control, he exerts his power through anger, intimidation, and abuse. The abuse can be verbal, emotional, physical, or sexual. If the home is structured along authoritarian lines, anger and expression of power often wipes out the expression of love so needed when differences occur in a family.

Words like "submission," "forgiving the abuser," "obey your parents," "the Bible says," "God says," become clubs that may keep people quiet when suffering abuse.

Because anger can be so uncomfortable and make us feel so out of control, many avoid anger at all costs. We don't admit we are angry. But anger will find its expression, often indirectly. For example, anger not expressed can lead to a shutdown of all feelings, even positive ones. This slowly kills a relationship.

Nursed hurts become destructive forces in relationships. They may explode when a person doesn't get the expected job promotion, when a husband doesn't "let" his wife go back to school, when children don't fulfill dreams parents have for them, when one loses a game.

Anger can be denied. Judith Viorst (1986, p. 250) describes such a scene in her book, *Necessary Losses*. She talks about family myths or themes of the harmonious, united family. Listen to the tone of the mother insisting (with her husband's full agreement) on the harmonious happiness of their home.

> We are all peaceful. I like peace even if I have to kill some-one to get it. . . . A more normal, happy kid would be hard to find. I was pleased with my child! I was pleased with my husband! I was pleased with my life! I have *always* been pleased! We have had 25 years of the happiest married life and of being a father and mother.

We have a "theology of nice" that can also hide a volcano of emotions. A pastor may be experiencing spiritual drought, problems in marriage, problems with children. But she or he cannot be honest about what is going on inside because the job requires, implicitly or explicitly, that everything be "fine." Pastors and their families are expected to be "nice" at all times.

Sally was a person like this. She was an attractive, smiling woman of thirty. She called one day insisting that she and her husband get help, because her husband had blown up at her, noting that he wished she would become real and let him know what she thought and felt. He was tired of niceness if all it meant was that she tried to make everything perfect. She was hurt and confused. Hadn't she been a good wife?

Sally came from a home in which there had been a lot of discord. Father, an alcoholic, was always angry. He would harass Mother until she was crying. The children could count on being punished with unpredictable regularity. Sally remembers a time when she was six that she heard her father beat her older brother. She says, "I hid, afraid he would beat me too." She remembers vowing to herself that when she grew up, she would never be angry like Dad. Her home would be different.

As we worked in therapy, at first she resisted any feelings of anger. Slowly she allowed herself to feel slight irritation, then hurt. One day she arrived in a crisis. She had become angry with her husband. Now what? Would her relationship be destroyed? Would the situation be out of control like Dad's anger was? As she continued with the therapy, she became aware of a large number of hurts, then a lot of angry feelings. Finally she became more comfortable with her own anger. She and her husband started to have disagreements. Curiously, she noted that she felt they loved each other more and that their relationship was improving.

Because anger can be so destructive, many Christians equate the feeling of anger with sin. However, the Bible does not take that position. Consider passages like Ephesians 4:26, James 1:19-20, and Matthew 21:18-22. What do these passages tell us about anger?

Anger is a natural emotion that, in itself, is not wrong. Here we can learn from the Psalms and Old Testament "heroes." The Hebrew tradition is filled with people who were angry with God, questioned God, complained to

God. *But* they always ended their tirade with an affirmation of God's grace, love, forgiveness, blessing, and their desired obedience to God's leading (see Psalms 7, 35, 58, 59, 69, 83, 109, 137, 140).

Anger is not only destructive. It can also be healing for relationships because it signals something that must be worked out, as in Sally's case. Often our best relationships are those in which anger was expressed and the issue resolved.

How does this work? Before we express anger we may need "time out." Clayton Barbeau, in the *Creating Family* film series, tells about a time their five-year-old was playing with matches. Barbeau was so upset and angry that he went to his room for about half an hour to cool off. When he came down, he told his child why he was so upset. He was reminded of his childhood when he was playing with matches and almost burned down their home.

In incidents where we lose control we must ask forgiveness of the person with whom we are angry. In the process of seeking forgiveness it is important that we address the issue that caused the anger. We have done what we believe is "Christian," but the response is up to the other person. The ideal is that a closer bond develops between us, but that may not always be possible immediately. It may depend on the other person's personal agenda. And it may take time and patience.

Learning to recognize and exercise those emotions in a healthy way helps, to a great extent, keep us mentally healthy. Experiencing the emotions does not make them right or wrong, it is what we do in the situations that evoke the emotions that creates healthy or unhealthy situations.

Welfare Emotions

One of the definitions we used for mental health at the beginning of this book was the evidence of the fruit of the

Spirit, God's influence in our lives. These were "love, joy, peace, patience, kindness, goodness, faithfulness, gentleness, self-control" (Gal. 5:22). Note that these are all, or can be, emotional responses to our human needs. They are what we might call "welfare emotions"—emotions that are a result of being at peace with God, ourselves, and others.

In Scripture welfare emotions are considered evidence of belonging to Jesus Christ (Gal. 5:24). They can help us meet the fray of the day. Think about how these "welfare emotions" could help us deal with destructive emergency emotions, such as anger and fear. Let's consider a few of these briefly.

Love. This is the basis for the connectedness to each other and to God. It always works for good, a community of people caring for each other. M. Scott Peck (1979, p. 81). defines love as, "The will to extend oneself for the purpose of nurturing one's own or another's spiritual growth." We could add physical, emotional, social, and *mental* growth.

Joy. Joy is the emotion which results from a solid love relationship. It is the feeling of ecstasy that, as Nouwen says, comes from living in the house of love, not the house of fear. This isn't necessarily the bubbly, gushy kind of happiness that comes out of our "theology of nice," but an inward optimism, *shalom.*

True joy is difficult in a world that wants everyone to "don't worry, be happy." It seems that when we have that inward optimism, we have the coping mechanism for dealing with difficult life situations. For Christians, the extra source of optimism comes through Christ, who came "that our joy might be full."

Peace. Peace is the freedom from conflict within oneself as well as with others. Again, peace comes from the security of being loved and from loving. It flourishes in relationship where there is trust. Peace is knowing that I am not a bad person, that God loves me even if I express my emergency emotions at seemingly inappropriate times.

Patience. We live our lives in pressured ways. We want it now, not tomorrow. Our emergency emotions may be a result of trying to solve life crises right now, in our way. Think of Jesus' mother, who wanted him to do something about the lack of wine at the wedding. Jesus' response? "My hour has not yet come" (John 2:4). Jesus often had to tell those around him that their concerns would be taken care of when the time was right.

In this age of immediate gratification, learning to be patient may be one of the best things we can do for our own and others' mental health.

Kindness. What effect does kindness have on us and our relationships? Active listening to the needs of others and responding to them with understanding and kindness can do wonders for persons in emotional turmoil. It may mean being angry, together, with the wife who is being abused by a controlling husband. It may also mean going shopping for the elderly person afraid of going out in the evening. These are only a few illustrations.

Goodness. Goodness has many different meanings. "Be a good boy." "That pie sure was good!" "She was a good speaker!" "That was a good sermon." In these illustrations, "good" is an adjective or adverb, labels put onto others or situations by people. As a fruit of the Spirit, it is a noun—a state of being, which means that it is part of one's being or personality.

Faithfulness. Faithfulness implies that one has a cause or belief system that guides one's actions and relationships. Jesus Christ is the ultimate example, from his baptism to his death on the cross. Looking at Christ's life, one doesn't get the impression that he was coerced into being who he was. He is the ultimate example of what it means to be faithful to one's mission in life.

Gentleness. Once again we look at Jesus' ministry, especially to the outcasts of Jesus' day. One example is the woman with the bleeding disorder. She was ritually un-clean. By touching his garment, Jesus was also "unclean" according to the law. What did he do? He spoke to her, calling her "daughter." That's gentleness.

If we are influenced by welfare emotions, our relation-ships will be gentle. We will even be gentle with ourselves. Question: If we can't be gentle with ourselves, can we be gentle with others?

Self-control. Throughout the biblical story, we find peo-ple judged, punished, and reprimanded for lack of self-control. Jesus' first temptations challenged his ability to control human needs like power, authority, greed, and submission to God, all issues of self-control. Unfortunate-ly, we are still confronted by persons and situations that challenge our self-control. One of the questions that arises in the context of this chapter is how one is able to exercise self-control, given one's living environment.

Note that Galatians 5:22 refers to "fruit," not "fruits." This implies that all of these welfare emotions are interre-lated. It is the connection between the emergency and wel-fare emotions in our personal lives that will determine, to a great extent, our mental health.

In this chapter we have alluded to emergency emo-tions resulting from fear and anxiety. This will be the focus for the next chapter.

For Further Study

1. How does Tevye, in *Fiddler on the Roof*, express his anger whenever he has to face change? How does he conclude his tirade against God?

For further insight on the Jewish tradition of emotional responses to God, consider the book by Elie Wiesel listed below. Wiesel provides a delightful, provocative insight into the biblical, Talmudic, and Hasidic traditions. What we, as Christians, might learn from Wiesel's stories, is how to complain to God and argue with God, yet have a reverence for God.

2. Discuss the connection between the fruit of the Spirit and mental health. Include specific examples to illustrate those connections.

3. What were you taught about dealing with the emergency emotions, as described in this chapter? In what way(s) does that agree or disagree with your view today?

4. What impression(s) do you get regarding emergency and welfare emotions? Can they be separated? If so, how? If not, why?

5. How are emotional responses to life situations affected by one's external environment? This environment can be family, school, work, church, community, nation.

6. What is the role of the church? Can people in the church understand the experiences that have shaped people dominated by emergency emotions?

7. What are the implications of this chapter for the congregation's ministry through the educational program, worship services, and pastoral care?

8. If I was hurting and came to your church, could I be open about it? Could I expect people to respond to me, my need, be gentle with me and support me? Discuss.

Additional Resources

Augsburger, David. *Caring Enough to Hear and Be Heard.* Scottdale: Herald Press, 1982.

Augsburger, David. *Caring Enough to Confront.* Scottdale: Herald Press, 1973.

Crabb, Lawrence J., Jr., and Allender, Dan. B. *Encouragement: The Key to Caring.* Grand Rapids: Zondervan, 1984.

Craven, Toni. *The Book of Psalms*. Collegeville: The Liturgical Press, 1992.

Huggett, Joyce. *Listening to Others*. London: Hodder and Stoughton, 1988.

Nouwen, Henri. *Lifesigns*. New York: Doubleday, 1989.

Peck, M. Scott. *The Road Less Traveled*. New York: Simon & Schuster, 1979.

Stanger, Frank Bateman. *God's Healing Community*. Francis Asbury Society, 1985.

Viorst, Judith. *Necessary Losses*. New York: Ballantine Books, 1986.

Wiesel, Elie. *Sages and Dreamers: Biblical, Talmudic, and Hasidic Portraits and Legends*. New York: Simon & Schuster, 1991.

Video:

Surviving Series with Clayton Barbeau (anger, broken relationships, difficult people, failure/rejection, grief). Available from the Conference of Mennonites in Canada Resource Centre (Winnipeg).

6

Who of You by Worrying Can Add a Single Hour to Your Life?

Scripture
Matthew 6:25-33

Opening Thoughts
The church is full of people who experience anxiety. For some anxiety is short-lived, for others it becomes immobilizing. Yet we are strangely silent about our anxieties.

In this chapter we look at what motivates and drives us and the disorders that can result from stress and anxieties.

Story
James is a twenty-three-year-old university student. He works hard at his studies. He is conscientious, serious, and dependable. His assignments are always done well ahead of time. In fact, he notes he can't really relax when he knows that there is work to be done.

He will never forget March 25, 1993. He had studied

hard for an examination. However, the questions were un-anticipated and he felt he had done poorly. He felt he should get right to work again but instead went to the mall just to walk around. As he was looking in the various shops, he began to notice that he was light-headed. He felt faint. James found a place to sit, but the feeling would not go away. Instead it intensified. Now there was ringing in his ears. His fingers became numb, then started to tingle. Then he noted that his fingers started to cramp.

This occurred over about three minutes. As it was hap-pening he began to feel an intense need to get out of the shopping center. He felt panic set in. As he tried to figure out what was happening to him, the thought flashed through his mind that he had a brain tumor. After all, this was the only thing that could explain how he was feeling.

Gradually the feeling subsided and he shakily went home. The next day it happened again. By now he was re-ally scared. He went to his family doctor, who tried to reas-sure him by ordering a lot of tests. This did not reassure him. Instead the fact that the tests were done convinced him something was wrong. When he was told that he was suffering from anxiety and panic he couldn't believe it. Could just plain anxiety be so bad?

Since then he has worried about it happening again. The fear is constantly on his mind. It has affected his stud-ies. He is always doubting that he can be successful. He has not returned to the shopping center. He tried to go to it about a week later but turned back at the door. He "knew" he would feel sick there again.

James is a Christian. He is now angry at himself for feeling this way. After all, didn't Christ tell us not to wor-ry? He feels he is failing as a Christian and hides the anxi-ety he feels. There is no one he feels he can talk with about it.

Focus

Christ asks us to not worry and not be anxious. After all, God will take care of us. Like James, many of us are filled with worries and anxieties, and a number of us also get panic attacks.

James' story is dramatic in that he had a panic attack that set off the anxiety symptoms. But when talking to him we would soon discover that he had always been a worrier. His life was lived with the "What if?" thoughts. For James life was an increasing set of anxieties.

A large study of the incidence of mental disorders completed in a number of cities in the United States shows that anxiety disorders are the most common of all mental disorders. Some people have anxiety symptoms so severe they would be called "disordered." Millions experience lesser degrees of anxiety. No one is immune from worries and anxiety.

Search

Let's try to understand stress as it affects anxieties.

The Stress Cycle

The physiologist Cannon noted that when animals are stressed they have one of two reactions. They either run away or prepare for battle.

Our response to stress isn't all that different. The animal perceives a threat and responds with bodily changes preparing for fight or flight. The perception of the threat comes through sensory inputs.

Our responses differ from animals in that we are capable of perceiving imagined, anticipated threats through our thoughts. This means that we have the ability to create problems for ourselves through these same thoughts.

The recognition of external threat occurs as either a

perception or a thought in the brain, where the threat is translated into our body through nerve impulses and various hormones. We experience bodily sensations such as muscle tension, agitation, a fast heart rate, perspiration, a knot in our stomach, weak knees, and hot and cold flashes. We can develop rapid breathing which can lead to a feeling of dizziness. Then vision starts to change. Hands start to tingle and may even slowly cramp.

The person with an anxiety attack feels something terrible is happening. It may feel like a heart attack, because there is discomfort in the chest, or a brain tumor, as in James' case, or simply a sense of "going crazy." All of these physiological signs make us more anxious, and we enter a vicious cycle of anxiety. This is the body prepared to battle or retreat from an unknown enemy. Our body doesn't know that we may be fighting our own mental ghosts.

What Makes Stress Worse?

To understand anxiety, we need to look at stressors that can cause it.

Severity. The more severe the stress, the greater its potential to make us dysfunctional.

Regularity. If the stresses come constantly, we eventually get to the stage where the body stress thermostat is set at high tension and anxiety all the time.

External stressors. We are pressured, or pressure ourselves, into hustling for money, possessions, and security. Once we get onto the treadmill of a fast-paced existence, it is difficult to change our style of life. External stressors can include work, unemployment, family relationships, retirement, parents who experience "empty nests," children during summer holidays, time demands. Expectations in the Christian community also contribute to the external stressors, the pressures ("shoulds") we place on ourselves or let others place on us.

Personality. Our own personalities may add stress to our lives. Personality and temperamental characteristics are at least in part genetically determined.

Some of us are stressed because we try to understand everything that happens. We are obsessed with rules and needing to know the "whys" in life—which only adds to stress.

Some of the most productive, though most stressed, people are those with obsessive compulsive personalities. Companies, organizations, and churches love these people because they are hardworking and dependable. They are often the workaholics. However, the price for all this obsessiveness is the loss of spontaneity or creativity necessary for growth and change in an organization, church, family, or business and may be personally harmful.

Internal expectations. As we grow up we take into ourselves our parent's expectations, culture, the teaching of the church, our understanding of biblical expectations. Christian beliefs are added to the expectations already internalized. This becomes our conscience.

Understanding the work of our conscience can be difficult and confusing. When guilt is felt is it the Holy Spirit? What I learned in the family, school, church or society? The expectations I have of myself? When we can't live up to those internal measures we respond with guilt and an incredible feeling of failure and worthlessness.

These stressors may not occur in isolation. A person can experience a combination of the stressors.

Results of Stress

In this section we will consider a few results of stress.

Burnout. A number of years ago I received a call late on a Friday afternoon. The man was choked, crying, and almost incoherent. He asked to see me immediately. When I did see him he revealed that he had been an exceptionally competent worker. That afternoon he had experienced one stress too many. He had been found by his co-workers sitting at his desk crying and aimlessly shifting papers around one after another.

After thirty years with the company he could not survive one more day. He went on sick leave, and I doubt he ever returned to the company. He explored other things he might do with his life. The pressure of always trying to meet demands took its toll.

Burnout can manifest itself in increasing feelings of inadequacy, loss of interest in the job, and not caring any more. As the saying goes, "If you hate going to work on Monday morning, you might need to consider a job change." Or we may notice we are doing more and more but accomplishing less.

Most of us are prone to burnout unless we balance the work we do with relaxation. Take another look at the rhythm of life in Ecclesiastes 3.

Disturbed relationships. Stress seldom affects only the stressed person. Carrying too big a load of stress will inevitably affect family or friends. The stressed-out person is likely to be short-tempered and irritable with others. We just need to talk to anyone in a helping profession or listen to a newscast to know the linkage between stress and family or work-related violence.

Psychosomatic conditions. Stress can initiate a wide range of physical problems such as high blood pressure, heart disease, ulcers, and bowel syndromes. There is even some thought that it predisposes people to cancer. We know that depression and anxiety states result from stress.

Alcohol and drug abuse. People abusing alcohol and drugs are not necessarily looking for a high. Instead they are trying to get rid of, or not feel, the tension and fear with which they live. This can lead to addictions which will be covered in another chapter.

Anxiety Disorders

In addition to the stress responses listed, a number of specific mental disorders have anxiety as a key feature and in part are associated with stress. The following are common anxiety disorders.

Generalized anxiety disorder. This person is anxious in the extreme for long periods of time. There is constant anxiety. The person is always on edge, irritable, and has trouble sleeping. These people look anxious, perspire, and tremble. They worry about everything. They may experience more specific symptoms like panic and phobias. In severe forms, people suffering from this disorder experience anxiety at all times.

Panic disorder. Nancy was putting a dish in the microwave oven when she suddenly felt that the microwave would explode. She went into a profound panic, ran out of the kitchen, and took a couple of hours to return.

Nancy was one of the most competent people one could ever meet and held a top job in the country. Competence does not protect from panic. She had another series of panics until finally she had to leave her job. It was a year before she was able to return to work.

Panic disorders are so disabling because, once we experience a panic, we try to avoid whatever triggered the panic. Panics come on suddenly and only last about twenty minutes, but they are the worst minutes of our life, until the next attack. They can be immobilizing even though we know there may not be a reason to fear the situation.

Phobias. Phobias are irrational fears of particular situations or things. Some phobias are quite restricted, such as fear of bees or flying. Others are much more general and can restrict one's life. Examples include a fear of germs or a fear of height.

Obsessive compulsive disorder. This disorder is an extreme form of what many of us are by personality. It may be the excessive need for rules, need to be a certain weight (leading to bulimia or anorexia), rituals (excessive need to wash hands) and so on.

How can this affect our faith? One example would be the obsessive compulsive who finds swear words coming to mind with every entry into church. The person knows that those thoughts are unacceptable in the church. As this continues, and if it increases, the situation can increase the level of stress to the point where the obsessive compulsive cannot relate to God or others in the church.

The Connection of Christian Faith and Anxiety

I am often amazed at how happy some people are who live very simply. Their lives show much enjoyment of simple pleasures. It is possible that these people experience less stress. We can decide to live more simply and less competitively, but that means going counter to everything we have been taught in our culture.

So where is the balance? Can we avoid the stresses coming from fears and anxieties and still be involved in life tasks? The Bible seems to suggest that the only way we can endure all of the pressures is to "seek first the kingdom of God." Given the content of this chapter, we can see that this may not be that simple.

Our faith may be used in healthy or unhealthy ways to deal with anxiety. On the "healthy" side, faith properly applied has a way of helping us look outside our situation to a Higher Being. We don't own the problem alone. The Christian faith and faith community can both be sources of support.

Harold Kushner (1989) describes the difference between the atheist and the one who believes in God when confronting difficulties. The atheist is like a sagebrush with shallow roots. As soon as difficulties come along, the atheist is uprooted and has to depend on the self. The one who believes in God is like the tree planted beside a stream, where the roots have a constant source of nourishment and support when difficulties come along.

As was mentioned in the chapter on life stages and mental health, trust, including the ability to trust God, begins to be learned at an early age. Growth, as well as nurture in the faith by the family and faith community, provide the root system for dealing with the normal fears and anxieties of life.

There are two promises that have become important when I get anxious. One is that "There is no fear in love, but perfect love casts out fear" (1 John 4:18).

The second promise is that "the one who is in you is greater than the one who is in the world" (1 John 4:4). The power in this verse tells me that I don't need to feel overwhelmed by all of the insecurities of life. The promises may not take the problems away, but they can help make problems easier to bear and master.

I have also found that, when I am anxious, it is helpful to pray out of the solution rather than the problem. What do I mean by that? When I am anxious my usual prayer is, "Lord, you've got to help me and you've got to help me right now." That comes close to manipulating God.

An important healing practice for this situation is found in Hebrews 13:15-16; "Through him, then, let us continually offer a sacrifice of praise to God, that is, the fruit of lips that confess his name. Do not neglect to do good and to share what you have, for such sacrifices are pleasing to God."

When we are pleading with God we are often feeding our anxieties and using prayer to ruminate on them. If instead we praise God, we are taking ourselves outside of the problem. So now we are not praying out of the problem anymore. We are praying out of the solution.

Note the last part of the passage, "Do not neglect to do

good and to share with others." When we are anxious we get too wrapped up in ourselves. The more we can focus on other people the better our handling of anxiety can be, because again we have shifted the focus outside of ourselves.

One of the people I spoke with told me that when she was really anxious she started to do things for others and the more she did things for other people the more she gained mastery over her anxiety and depression. She was dealing with the solution, not the problem. She was taking herself out of the problem by focusing on others.

An unhealthy faith can make anxiety worse. This is part of the external stressors we discussed earlier. What about fears and anxiety that come from concerns about our spiritual life, our relationship with God?

Two books provide serious food for thought when considering the need for pastors and congregations to examine the theology and possible spiritual abuse in the church—*Faith That Hurts, Faith That Heals* and *The Subtle Power of Spiritual Abuse* (cited in the resources section). Out of their pastoral and counseling experiences, the authors offer disturbing descriptions of the misuse and abuse of Scripture and power in the context of the Christian church. Many fears and anxieties faced by persons in the church are caused by shame and further pressures placed on vulnerable and weak persons. A key question the authors raise is whether the Christian faith community helps or hinders persons' needs for healing and understanding, especially when it comes to spiritual matters.

Help with Anxiety

There are additional ways of helping relieve anxiety. Some are listed below. It must be noted that severe cases of fear and anxiety will most likely require professional help.

Relaxation. Psychologists have noted that we can't be relaxed and anxious at the same time. One form of relaxation is the use of relaxation tapes that help us voluntarily relax muscle groups. The theory is that if our muscles are relaxed, we will be relaxed.

Meditation. Christians have a powerful tool for relaxation in prayer and meditation. Meditation is a twofold process. It is active in that we must determine to meditate. It is passive in that we allow ourself to relax in the presence of God. People who schedule quiet times regularly invariably speak about how refreshed they feel.

Face your fears and anxieties. Avoiding the situation that causes the anxiety only prolongs or worsens the battle with anxiety. The road to recovery becomes increasingly hard. The healing process can begin when we face fears and anxieties. This is where family, friends, the faith community, and dependence on God can play a vital part.

Thought blocking. There are certain things we cannot allow ourselves to think about because we get too anxious. These are especially situations or events over which we have no control. This also includes taking others' problems as our own.

As a means of thought blocking, I sometimes tell my patients to select specific verses with specific promises and read them repeatedly, especially the promises of hope and healing.

Reality testing. Our anxieties seldom have anything to do with reality. When we are anxious we are sure that the worst will happen. Sure it may, but the chances are much greater that the worst may never happen. One idea is to write down fears and anxieties. Next, write beside each one, what the worst thing is that could happen as a result of that fear or anxiety. What can be controlled and what cannot be controlled?

Doing this exercise may be the major step in determining what is real and what is imagined. It may also lead to the point where we can decide whether this can be handled by the individual or group, or whether there is a need for professional consultation.

Avoid being a slave to time. Many fears and anxieties come as a result of overscheduling ourself and stretching beyond what can be accomplished realistically. Ecclesiastes 3 talks about the rhythm of life. Note question 2 in the For Further Study section.

Avoid substances. Anxiety attacks may come as a result of overloading on addictive substances like caffeine. This may be difficult for the coffeeholic, chocoholic, and colaholic to hear, but we must be aware that anxiety is often our body's response to caffeine. Addictions are discussed in chapter eight.

Medication. Some people need medication. At a crisis point drugs may help persons move through the toughest period until they can manage a little better and face their problems in other ways. Christians are human and may also need medication.

However, the danger comes with increasing dependence on the beautiful pills that give "a moment of peace" in people who are chronically anxious. Professional input from a doctor or pharmacist is highly recommended when determining the need for drugs, whether over-the-counter or prescription.

Look for support. We don't need to go it alone. Support groups inside and outside the faith community are available to help persons deal with fears and anxieties. One of the keys is to find support systems that empathize and struggle with us *and* are honest in telling us when they cannot deal with our problems. God may be using our support systems to tell us when to look for professional help.

For Further Study

1. At the beginning of the chapter have participants list as many situations as possible that cause anxieties.

2. Clayton Barbeau, in the *Creating Family* film series, frequently makes the comment, "Where you place your time you place your life, and where you place your life you place your love." How could this thought diminish fears and anxieties?

3. Reflect on ways parents can deal with stresses without putting themselves on "guilt trips."

4. Consider Matthew 14:23; Mark 1:35; 6:46; Luke 5:16; 6:12; 9:18; 9:28. What do we learn from Jesus' life that could help reduce fears and anxieties?

5. How can the faith community's understanding of psychological disorders enable ministry to the whole person?

6. Discuss the role of the professional (psychologist, psychiatrist, pastor) in dealing with the issues in this chapter.

7. How can a worship service speak to fears and anxieties faced by persons of all ages on a Sunday morning?

8. Look at the announcement section of the church bulletin on a Sunday morning. What events or programs would enable anxieties (increase situations causing anxieties) and which would lower anxieties? (Consider age groups, marital status, lifestyles, life need in your response.)

Additional Resources

Arturburn, Stephen and Felton, Jack. *Faith That Hurts, Faith That Heals*. Nashville: Oliver-Nelson Publishers, 1993.

Hanson, Peter G. *The Joy of Stress*. Hanson Stress Management Organization, 1986.

Johnson, David and VanVonderen, Jeff. *The Subtle Power of*

Spiritual Abuse. Minneapolis: Bethany House Publishers, 1991.

Kushner, Harold. *Who Needs God.* Toronto: Summit Books, 1989.

Linn, Matthew; Fabricant, Sheila; and Linn, Dennis. *Healing the Eight Stages of Life.* New York: Paulist Press, 1988.

Worthington, Everett L. *How to Help the Hurting: When Friends Face Problems with Self-Esteem, Self-Control, Fear, Depression, Loneliness.* Downer's Grove: InterVarsity Christian Press, 1985.

Video:

Living with Stress. Dr. Donald Tubesing explores how Christians can/should relate to stress. Thirty minutes.

7

My God, My God, Why Have You Forsaken Me?

Scripture

Psalm 22; Psalm 38

Opening Thoughts

When we think of depression in spiritual terms, the words of Psalm 22 ("My God, my God, why have you forsaken me?") come to mind. The experience of severe depression is so painful that both Christians and those who do not share the faith often respond to depression with the fear that God has left them. Depression involves feeling lack of hope and total isolation.

Within the church many people have experienced depression. In every church there are people right now who are depressed; life for them is difficult. Often depression is seen by people in the church as a spiritual problem. In fact, I have come across material that basically states that if you get right with God, you will not be depressed. Is this so? Let's look at depression more closely.

Story

Pat's first depression occurred when she was twenty-five, just after her first child was born. The depression was mild and passed in a few months. Four years later, after the second child was born, she experienced another post-partum depression. This was more severe and didn't pass as quickly. She slept poorly and was always tired. She dreaded her husband's going to work in the morning and in part resented it because that left her with the children. She felt isolated and began to resent having stopped work to have the children.

As the feelings of anger increased, Pat began to feel a spiritual aspect to the depression. Surely there must be a spiritual problem or she would not feel as badly. She dealt with these feelings by joining a women's Bible study group. After some months the depression started to lift as she concentrated on her faith.

Her next depression started seven years later and lasted about six years but was not recognized as depression because she had physical symptoms. She noted pain in her stomach after eating. First she could eat no salads. Then other things were added to the list until finally she could eat little. She slowly lost weight. Trips to the doctor were frustrating because she was always told that nothing was wrong. However, she was convinced something was terribly wrong.

Again she turned to her faith and, in her words, "became more spiritual." She became a Sunday school superintendent and deacon. She felt driven. She knew if she could give God her all she would feel better. So, in an attempt to discover where she was failing, she examined her commitment to God. She reasoned, Who is the most holy? The pastors. They give their whole life to God.

So off to seminary she went. But she quickly discovered seminary was not for her. Now she was in a real dilemma. To be at home with her children was tough, and she always dreamed of what she would do when they became older. Now she had time and could follow her dreams, but nothing came. She could not get the energy or drive to do anything.

During this time her stomach problems grew worse and she restricted her food intake more. She began to feel she had cancer and was confused when the doctors again found nothing. She went to numerous charismatic healing services, but while they gave hope, nothing happened with her basic condition.

Pat continued to get worse. She felt hopeless and sad. She couldn't sleep and was again losing weight. The spiritual battle became dominant as she felt the hopelessness of pleasing God. Then she began to think of suicide. If this was all life was, maybe it was better ended. The suicidal thoughts took shape. She started to fantasize about having an accident with the car. These thoughts scared her. Finally she decided to see a psychiatrist.

Pat's own description of how she felt is revealing. "I couldn't make decisions, and this was different for me. I wasn't sad, just numb. I felt I couldn't live like this. I was so tired. I couldn't sleep. I was driving the car one day and I thought how nice it would be to drive into the river. I felt our marriage was no good. I didn't want him touching me. I felt horrible and guilty."

The psychiatrist spoke with her and prescribed antidepressant medication. Three weeks later Pat noticed she was beginning to feel better. She began to feel energy and hope. She had lost a lot of weight but now she was hungry. It was like heaven to eat again, and her stomach pains disappeared. There has been steady improvement since.

Focus

One problem with words is that they can mean different things to different people. The term *depression* has many meanings. This creates difficulties for us as we discuss depression, because we must be sure we are in agreement on terms.

Depression can mean a temporary low mood, like having a "blue day" or feeling momentary unhappiness. Or depression can mean a marked lowering of mood for a longer time accompanied by a whole series of physical and psychological symptoms much as Pat experienced.

The temporary disappointment or low mood is best thought of as unhappiness and not depression. This is a passing state likely caused by some experience. For example, a person whose business fails will not be happy, and the unhappiness may last for some time. But though unhappy, this person may not be depressed. Or the person who loses a loved one will be grieving but may not be depressed. Or, more trivially, a person who is having a bad day with a lot of disappointments or stresses may not be happy but again will not be depressed.

For depression to be present in the above situations, there must be a combination of psychological and physical symptoms. The physical symptoms are called the vegetative symptoms of depression. These are symptoms such as low energy, tiredness, loss of appetite, weight loss, loss of sex drive, constipation, difficulty sleeping (particularly waking early in the morning) and slow thinking. In fact, every aspect of such people's lives appears slowed down. Sometimes people complain of a multitude of aches and pains.

Sometimes there is a reversal of some of these symptoms. Some will eat a lot, gain weight, and sleep a lot in an attempt to feel better and avoid the pain of depression.

Psychologically, people with depression describe feeling empty inside or numb. Characteristically they speak of a feeling of despair, guilt, or hopelessness. There is often a feeling of dread. Christians feel as if God has forsaken them.

People with depression report that early mornings are the worst time of the day. They find themselves tossing in bed with no possibility of sleep while battling the unseen forces of fear and despair. Evenings are best, because there is the slight hope that the next day will be better. Unfortunately, the next day isn't any better.

Suicidal thoughts are common in depression, as people grapple with the feelings of hopelessness and long for release from what they feel.

Depression may come suddenly or gradually. It may last for days, weeks, months, and sometimes even years. However, for most people, even without treatment the depression will ultimately lift. It can, however, return.

Depression is relatively common, affecting up to 8 percent of the population at some time in life. We encounter depression in ourselves, families, friends, and people with whom we worship.

Search

It is important that we understand depression and especially how it relates to a life of faith.

Barry, age thirty-five, is a committed Christian, married for ten years and father of two children. In his early twenties, before he was married, he had a brief sexual relationship with a university classmate. He was bothered by it at the time and sought forgiveness for it from the young woman. He also confessed it to his Inter-Varsity Christian Fellowship leader.

He thought he had dealt with it. Two months ago the guilt returned. He is bothered by the thought that he can't be a good husband because he has sinned. He keeps asking his wife for forgiveness until she is tired of hearing it. He prays daily for forgiveness and feels God has not heard him. He tries to live a perfect life, but each day he finds areas where he could have been better and more "acceptable to God."

He does not sleep well, awakening often in the night. As he lies awake he feels his wife should leave him and he deserves it. Because he doesn't sleep well, he is tired. Food has lost its flavor. Pleasures have no appeal.

He visits his pastor, seeking spiritual assurance. But no assurance is good enough.

You can see how easy it would be for Barry to feel he had a spiritual problem. In fact, at first his wife thought so too, as did the pastor. After considerable discussions, his wife and pastor began to see he was depressed. However, Barry could not accept this. After all, he "knew" it was a spiritual problem.

People who are depressed want others to judge them for their spiritual inadequacies. They feel they deserve our criticism and condemnation. They believe they aren't pleasing God. Repeatedly they try to pull themselves out of the pit, but this effort helps for only a short time, and they enter the pit again.

Depression is recognized in the Bible. Tradition says that Psalm 22 was written by David when he was being pursued by his enemies and they were camped round about him. A difficult situation such as David experienced often precedes depression. One can feel with David's anguish. I don't think it is any coincidence that this psalm is quoted by Christ on the cross, when Christ says, "My God, my God, why have you forsaken me?"

If there is any feeling that sums up depression it is the feeling that one has been forsaken by God.

Remember, one of the psalms that speaks of being forsaken includes these beloved words: "Even though I walk through the darkest valley, I fear no evil; for you are with me" (Psalm 23). In his normal state the psalmist can trust in God, but in depression he feels abandoned.

Often when I see depressed Christians I comment, "So, it feels like God has packed his bags and gone away." They usually respond that that is exactly how it feels. Deep down they know God is there. They have been told God is there and they believe it on one level. But on another level they feel God has abandoned them.

It is reassuring that the Scriptures contain examples of depression, because we can identify with many of those experiences, "Ah, it has been felt before." This is particularly true of the Psalms.

Depression is also found in the story of Job. His life is often used as an example of extreme depression because of the difficulties he encountered. When his friends came to see him they kept trying to tell him what was sensible in their eyes. This just didn't wash with Job for two reasons. First, Job was working out his relationship with God in his own way. Second, when a person is depressed or going through a trying time, a friend may miss where the sufferer is at, making the situation worse because it increases isolation.

What Causes Depression?

Years ago depressions were classified in terms of whether the depression followed a definite life situation, such as a loss. Counselors felt that depressed persons who could name a definite situation causing their depression would respond better to counseling. If we can identify a reason, we feel we understand it more. We become frustrated with someone who is depressed and can't say why.

Researchers agree that a loss of some kind—a broken relationship, loss of a job, or a death—are factors that predispose us to depression. Whether or not stresses that cause depression are present, depression may still occur. Also, different people who experience similar events may not respond with depression at all. So events alone are not always likely to cause depression.

Scientists tell us that there is a genetic predisposition to depression that is inherited. This does not mean that children of a depressed parent will get depressed. All it means is that they have a greater likelihood of also getting depressed at some time in their lives.

Depression sometimes accompanies other physical illnesses like viral infections or cancer and may last long after the illness has passed.

There seem to be a multitude of factors working together that produce a depression. It is known that once persons have had one depression, there is a 60 to 70 percent chance that they will have another depression at some time. Depression often starts in adolescence or young adulthood, so many people carry the tendency to get depressed for much of their lives.

There is another troubling aspect to depression. The number of people who experience depression is increasing rapidly, particularly among adolescents and children.

What Happens in Depression?

In a previous chapter we discussed the bio-psycho-social model. How does it apply to depression? In the church we tend to think that depression is evident when one is pessimistic and has other negative thoughts and that these thoughts are what cause the sleep, energy, and appetite problems. We often hear or read that if persons would just think differently they would not be depressed.

This becomes a source of guilt for those who are depressed because often they try to think differently but they can't. Thinking differently, while it is important, is often not sufficient for a person to feel not depressed.

In one of the first chapters we noted that the brains of people who have committed suicide have a lower level of the substance serotonin than the normal population. Many people who do commit suicide are depressed. In recent years we have developed techniques for understanding what happens biochemically in the human brain. It is now known that serotonin levels are low in people who are depressed, as are other mood-sustaining chemicals. Antidepressant medication reverses these low levels, and the person ceases to be depressed.

The social isolation depressed people feel becomes a vicious cycle, because they spend too much time alone in which they can think about themselves and how miserable they feel.

Bipolar Disease

Knowing the variations in depression is important. One is the condition that used to be called manic-depression, now called bipolar disease.

Bipolar disease is characterized by periods of mania or high mood which may quickly shift into irritability, anger, or irrationality. People with mania think so rapidly that their thoughts may be disorganized. Sleep is a problem in that they have too much energy to sleep. They start many tasks but often don't accomplish much because they are too easily distracted. They lack good judgment and tend to spend large amounts of money, often money they don't have.

Sometimes bipolar disease becomes more chronic, with depression and manic episodes alternating frequently. This mood fluctuation makes it difficult to build any stability in life. The pattern is exceptionally hard on family members who, like the person who is ill, require a great deal of support. Bipolar disease is often controlled effectively by continuous use of mood-stabilizing medication.

Bob, an accountant, was always a conservative fellow in his habits, spending, and faith. He was a pillar in the church. He had experienced several depressions in the past, but they were not severe, and the people in the church did not notice them. One Sunday they noticed a change in Bob. He was more outgoing than usual. In fact, he was loud and a bit argumentative. He spoke rapidly.

This continued for a few weeks until Bob's wife called friends from the church for help. Bob had planned to donate all their savings to a TV ministry devoted to "endtimes" prophecy. He had been banging on neighbors' doors in the middle of the night, telling them to wake up for the end was near. The police had been called and asked him to be quiet.

He agreed, but shortly after they left, he became angry at his wife for not understanding. She felt she could not get through to him.

After some consultation, Bob's friends decided to take him to the local hospital, where he was admitted. In his case medication helped him return to normal. There has been no recurrence of the disease in four years.

Suicide

Suicide occurs with increased frequency in depressed people. Suicide is born out of the hopelessness and desperation people feel. When someone you know is depressed it is important to continue to be available to him or her. If there are any doubts about the person's safety, it is important to ask if the individual feels life is worth living or whether thoughts of self-harm are present. Asking will not increase the risk of suicide. Instead, it is usually seen as an offer of help.

The church through the centuries has seen suicide as wrong. Often persons who committed suicide were not permitted to have a church funeral or be buried in the church cemetery. Fortunately there is now more understanding about suicide and its causes. However, rarely is a church prepared for suicide when it happens. Each situation needs to be dealt with sensitively and openly. Both family members and the church community need to be involved in coming to terms with the suicide.

Help for Depression

Despite the feelings of hopelessness, there are things individuals, family, friends, and the church can do for depressed persons.

First, the individual can work on the depressive thoughts. There is an approach to depression called cognitive therapy. If depressing thoughts contribute to our depression, it follows that thinking realistic, more positive thoughts can help us with depression, as was mentioned earlier. This general approach is supported by Philippians 4:8, "Whatever is true . . . pleasing . . . think about these things." Often persons with mild depression will find comfort from this approach. They can be helped to change their thought patterns.

I also ask people who are mildly depressed to act as if they are not depressed, to go out, do things, and be with people. This will help them feel better, at least for the time they are active. But if someone is moderately or severely depressed this approach does not help much, since they just can't seem to get themselves going. In fact, they often interpret the pushing of well-meaning people as further evidence of their failure. Then they feel worse.

Depressed people will try to read the Bible, expecting it will help them experience peace. It may have the opposite effect. For example, the depressed person could read Isaiah 44:22, "I have swept away your transgressions like a cloud, and your sins like a mist; return to me, for I have redeemed you." The mildly depressed person may draw comfort from this, while the moderately depressed person may cling to it as an element of faith but with little comfort.

Depressed people tend to read judgment and failure in the Bible. Characteristically, they could interpret this verse, "This is so, but I have not 'returned' to the Lord. I have not repented enough of my sins. God is judging me." Reading a selected devotional book with purely positive content may be more helpful than reading the Bible since, like iron to a magnet, their eyes will turn to passages of judgment rather than grace.

While it is good for depressed people to be with people, going to church is often difficult because the content of the service may increase their guilt due to their vulnerability to guilt feelings. If church is a problem, it may be more beneficial to the person to meet with a small group of friends or even a caring individual instead. It is important that the depressed person's guilt about not being in church not be increased by insensitive comments.

Depressed persons need to see a health care professional. There are specific therapies that can help, like antidepressant medication. Often Christians resist the medication because they feel it is a crutch, an indication that they are weak. Or they fear that the medication is addictive (which is not the case). Another therapy that might be lifesaving is electro-shock therapy.

There are a number of other helpful specific psychological therapies for depression including counseling. The type of therapy required depends on the individual need, therefore it is vital that a professional be consulted.

What About the Church?

The following are a few suggestions for the faith community.

Support. The depressed person feels very isolated,

therefore, being with that person, offering support, giving encouragement and hope will help cut down the isolation of depression. Frequent brief visits tend to help most, as longer visits may be exhausting for the person. Remember, the caregivers also need support.

Understanding. It is easy to become impatient with the depressed person. We reason that if they would just try harder they would feel better. Pushing, prodding, preaching are not appropriate at these times. If gentle encouragement does not help, it is likely the person doesn't have the energy or motivation to get going. Pushing adds to the guilt and isolation.

Caregivers need to be reminded that the experiences of the depressed person are *their* experiences. This may be one of the most difficult roles of the caregiver—to *try* to understand the depressed person's experience. Supporting caregivers in what they do to help the depressed person to get help, may be the best kind of understanding we can give.

Depressed persons often try to trap caregivers in commenting on their failure or guilt. They try to get the caregiver to agree with them. Getting drawn into these critical comments may increase the depressed person's misery. Remember the comments of Job's friends.

Prayer. Prayer is essential in helping people who are depressed, because they may believe that God has abandoned them. However, the timing is crucial when introducing God or prayer, because the depressed person may be too despairing or angry at God. Might this timing also be necessary when considering the needs of the caregiver?

One sensitivity is to know when prayer is to be joint or private. The caregiver's prayer may need to be private because the depressed person may not find prayer comforting. There may be times others need to carry the faith for the depressed person and/or the caregiver.

Growth. Some people who have experienced depression find a new perspective on life as a result of their depression. They use this experience to focus on what is important and to concentrate on enjoying their life as a gift. Sometimes an experience like depression is used for psychological and spiritual growth.

For Further Study

1. What insights about depression come from the Scripture passages cited at the beginning of the session? Discuss the images and feelings in Psalm 22.

2. If there are persons in your group who have experienced periods of depression, and they are comfortable with sharing it, have them share their experience of how they got through their illness.

3. What triggers depression? Are there different situations at different points in one's life journey? How does this affect one's attitude toward aging?

4. What do you think about suicide? Is it wrong? Do you know anyone who has attempted suicide? How have attitudes toward suicide changed during your lifetime? How do you feel about them?

5. In what ways do our thoughts help or hinder our attitude toward the events of life? Share experiences of how changing thought patterns changed life situations.

6. What are some of the myths and attitudes toward therapies for treating mental illnesses, such as medications, electro-shock, etc.? If possible, have a mental health professional help you process some of your questions and fears about these therapies.

7. Discuss the point that there may be times when we have to have faith for others. How do we "carry" the depressed person? What are the implications for ourselves and our mental health?

8. Discuss the suggestions on the role of the church. What would you add to the points made in this session?

9. What questions do you still have regarding depression? Where might you find the resources to gain insights in response to those questions?

Additional Resources

Carr, G. Lloyd and Carr, Gwendolyn C. *The Fierce Goodbye: Hope in the Wake of Suicide.* Downer's Grove: InterVarsity Press, 1990.

Hart, Archibald D. *Coping with Depression in the Ministry and Other Helping Professions.* Dallas: Word, 1984.

Knowles, Jeffrey J. *What of the Night? A Journey Through Depression and Anxiety.* Scottdale: Herald Press, 1993.

Lockley, John. *A Practical Workbook for Depressed Christians.* Milton Keynes: Word (U.K.), 1991.

Timmerman, John H. *A Season of Suffering: One Family's Journey Through Depression.* Portland: Multnomah Press, 1987.

White, John. *The Masks of Melancholy.* Downer's Grove: InterVarsity Press, 1983.

Video:

Nobody Knows. An informative look at depression. The church and Christian faith are viewed appreciatively in the therapeutic alliance. Nineteen minutes.

8

No Other Gods

Scripture:
Romans 7:7-25; Exodus 20: 1-5

Opening Thoughts

Several different titles were considered for this chapter—"Substance Abuse" or "Drugs and Alcohol." Both of these titles address serious mental health problems which have implications for faith. However, a chapter on addictions in general should be more helpful.

What is the difference? Drugs and alcohol cause addictions. In the church many of us are affected by a broader range of addictions. We drink too much coffee and we overeat. We become addicted to work, considering it a virtue, and to certain pleasures and habits. In fact, some of us are addicted to our religion. Addiction affects all of us in many different ways. It may be more comfortable for us just to consider alcohol and drug addiction but it will be more helpful, in this chapter, to include a general discussion of addictions.

Story

The people at Hope Church left the Sunday morning worship service in stunned silence. Jerry, a deacon, had requested time to speak to the congregation. He revealed that he had just returned from an addiction treatment center, where he had received treatment for alcoholism. He told them that he was an alcoholic and had been for some years. He asked forgiveness for betraying the trust they had in him and offered his resignation as a deacon until he felt he was more secure in his recovery.

Jerry recounted his story. He started drinking when he was studying law. He came from a family where there were strict rules against alcohol, so he kept the drinking quiet. He managed to do well in university despite the fact that he often drank excessively. The pressures of studying, articling, establishing a practice in a large firm, and becoming a partner in the firm all took their toll. He worked compulsively. He could not sleep, so he drank nightly until he fell asleep.

He married his high school sweetheart in his final year of law school. She did not approve of his drinking but reasoned that he was under a lot of pressure and would stop once he joined a law firm. She colluded with him not to speak about his drinking to others, as she felt it would damage his reputation and lessen his chances for success. Their marriage gradually deteriorated, although to see them together in church one would never guess it. Jerry was active in church, rapidly becoming one of the leaders.

In the last year Jerry had started drinking at noon, over lunch. One day he returned to the office intoxicated and was sent home. He stopped his lunch drinks for a month, then started again. One afternoon his secretary noticed he was intoxicated again. That afternoon he made a serious error in dealing with a client's file. She spoke to the senior partner and the partner insisted that Jerry receive treatment. Jerry let people know that he was going on vacation and quietly entered treatment. In the treatment center Jerry started to face himself for the first time. His wife also received counseling and together they learned about the collusions they had formed and the lies they lived.

As part of Jerry's recovery he felt it important to speak to the church. The question now is, How will they receive his news? Will they still accept him?

Focus

All of the elements of addiction are present in Jerry's story. Here is a person who is vulnerable to addiction and the thing (alcohol in Jerry's case) to which one is addicted. There is an environment characterized by denial and cover-up that allows the addiction to continue undetected until a crisis comes along. This crisis often takes longer to surface because there is an "enabler," (like Jerry's wife) who doesn't confront the addiction but hopes it will go away by itself. More about this later.

Alcohol and drug dependency has been termed a disease. This view has been instrumental in reducing the stigma associated with the condition and legitimizing treatment for it. At the same time that it is considered a disease, others consider it a moral problem and see in the disease concept an evasion of moral responsibility. The reasoning is that if persons were determined enough and the relationship with God right, victory would quickly follow. Stories exist of people who have become Christians almost instantaneously losing all desire to drink. However, others in the same situation struggle with the problem for years.

If this tension between addiction as a disease or a spiritual issue is present in the visible addictions like drugs and alcohol, it follows that the same considerations exist for the quieter, more hidden addictions to food, sex, pleasure, work, security. Now I can hear some saying, "But these aren't addictions like the others." This may be so, as each addiction has its own unique characteristics. However, in recent years there has been increasing awareness that addiction is a general problem, affecting people in many areas of their lives.

In this chapter we will first need to consider certain points addictions have in common. This might be considered the disease model. Then we will consider the spiritual aspect of addictions. Finally we will discuss what might be done about the problem of addictions as experienced by the individual, the family, and the church.

Search

Webster's dictionary definition of "to be addicted" is "to devote or surrender to something habitually or compulsively." Addiction is defined by Gerald May (1988) as, "Any compulsive, habitual behavior that limits the freedom of human desire" (p. 24). May's definition implies that we were made for freedom and in the state of addiction we are enslaved. Both of these definitions do not state the substances, things, acts, or attitudes necessary for us to be addicted. Presumably it could be a wide range.

Addiction
Substance Addiction

Addictions have certain features in common. The first is that one becomes dependent on the addictive agent. Consider alcohol. At first the person may drink alcohol because it is enjoyable. Then the body starts to demand alcohol because alcohol has created a demand for itself in the body. As the person's body becomes tolerant of a certain level of alcohol, more is required to produce the same effect. If there is a great deal of dependency and no available alcohol, the addicted person goes through withdrawal effects that, left untreated, carry a risk of death.

After the initial release one feels while drinking, the depressive phase of alcohol clicks in. The person may then feel depressed, angry, or irritable. Judgment is also impaired. This tends to lead to interpersonal and social crises that compound the bad emotional effects of alcohol. In fact, many suicide attempts are influenced, in part, by alcohol.

Alcohol is a model for addictions to other substances. A substance foreign to the body sets up a physical dependency in the body that demands regular use of the drug to prevent withdrawal.

Use of illegal drugs produces the same effects, often with even more social problems that derive from the high cost of the street drugs.

However, we don't have to look just on the dark, illegal side of life. People become addicted to prescription tranquilizer drugs like Valium, Librium, and others.

Nicotine in cigarettes also sets up an addictive pattern, with physical dependency which makes it hard to stop smoking, even in the face of potential emphysema and lung cancer.

There are additional substance addictions that are mild but still represent a potential problem, such as addiction to caffeine in coffee or tea. It used to be thought that there was no withdrawal from caffeine, but we now know that there is a definite withdrawal characterized by hot and cold flashes and headaches. Usually a coffee drinker knows that he or she requires the cup or two in the morning to start the day.

Drive Addictions

A number of addictions are not caused by adding a foreign substance to our bodies but arise, instead, from indulging our drives to relieve anxiety or to feel good. An example in this category is addiction to food, such as habitually overeating or being addicted to certain kinds of food.

An extreme example of a drive addiction is the condition known as bulimia, where the person who is addicted gorges on high calorie food, becomes worried about how much has been eaten, then vomits or takes laxatives to eliminate the food. The cycle repeats itself.

Another addiction may be to sexual activity. One wonders if the ready availability of adult videos and other pornographic material contributes to hidden addictions of persons in the church.

Attraction Addictions

Gerald May (1988) provides another way of looking at addictions—*attraction* addictions and *aversion* addictions.

Attraction addictions arise out of attraction to a specific thing. For example, it is possible to have an addiction to money or to security. We are only comfortable if we have money available or if we are absolutely secure, but we never have enough.

Other addictions may be to being good, helpful, or nice to guarantee love.

That is not to say that the objects of all these addictions are wrong. It would be ludicrous to discourage being good. However, the motive for the goodness determines whether it is part of an addiction.

Addiction to religion is another form of attraction addictions. In this instance the person is addicted to the form and practice of the religion rather than God.

May lists additional attraction addictions, such as needing to be considered attractive, being taken care of, cars, causes, competition, dreams, exercise, family, guilt, intimacy, sports heroes, music. None of these are bad in themselves. But when they become a habit that must be indulged, they become an addiction.

Aversion Addictions

There are also aversion addictions. Here the aversion is so strong we can't shake it. It preoccupies much of our time. The addiction is often represented by our fears or our dislikes. The difference between normal fear and addiction is that normal fear is recognized and dealt with, whereas addiction goes on and on, preoccupying us when there is no reason.

When we considered anxiety disorders, we noted that phobias are the unrealistic fears of situations or things that have to be avoided. Another way of looking at phobias and other strong dislikes is as aversion addictions.

Now I can imagine you saying, "Hold on now, you're not talking about addictions any more. You're talking about life in general."

Tolerance and Withdrawal

In each addiction one can recognize the person gradually developing tolerance, until the addiction begins to define life.

We know that the addictions we first considered—alcohol and drugs—carry with them bodily changes or physiological dependence. It is now suggested by researchers that in these addictive preoccupations certain connections get "hard-wired" into the brain. As well, with these addictions there is evidence of anxiety engendered by withdrawal from the addiction if the person is prevented from fulfilling the need for the addicting agent. This is all in keeping with the definitions of addiction with which we started this chapter.

Denial and Codependency

Denial and codependency are means of supporting addictions by not recognizing them, often when they are painfully obvious to others. This was touched on earlier but will be developed more fully here.

Denial. One of the most powerful forces in allowing an addiction to become established and to continue is the psychological defense of denial. Here the person and family fail to notice, until quite late, that all of the signs of the addiction are there and should be addressed. The addicted person always seems to have full control and to be able to stop at any time. Excuses are made to explain and rationalize behavior whenever questioned or confronted about the addiction.

Codependency. The addict usually does not exist alone. We saw how Jerry's wife protected him from exposure. In some ways, her role was to protect him so his addiction would not come to light. So often the spouse, family member, or co-worker of the addicted person protects, makes excuses, cares for the person, and in many ways allows the addiction to continue.

We have become increasingly aware that often for addicts to stop their addiction, spouses (or enablers) of addicted persons must examine why they participate in helping the addiction continue. Often it is out of their own needs to be a care-taker, to be "needed," fear of change, or other personal need. Codependents must come to realize that often the most loving thing that can be done for addicted persons is to stop supporting them. Tough love is hard, costly, and painful. Groups like ALANON have formed specifically to help the spouses of alcoholics gain support and deal with codependency that perpetuates the addiction.

As more is learned about codependency, more assistance is available for the codependent person.

Is Addiction a Disease or a Spiritual Issue?

Traditionally in our churches addiction has been seen as a spiritual issue. More recently the disease concept of addiction has been promoted. Are these two positions at cross-purposes? Or can addiction be both a spiritual issue and a disease?

The spiritual side of addiction is seen in the two Bible readings for this chapter. The passage from Exodus (20:1-5) is the commandment to have no other gods but God. Israel as a people was called to radical monotheism. God alone was to be worshiped. But what does that have to do with addiction?

Gerald May (1988) notes that addiction is wrong because it is idolatry. Something other than God has become the object of desire and controls our life. Remember that, in the definition of addiction that we considered earlier in this chapter, May notes that addiction limits the freedom of human desire. It follows that God wishes to be the object of our desire, rather than have us enslaved to other, lesser things.

What do you think about the concept of addiction as idolatry? Does it fit or is it overstating a case? My first reaction to this material was that it was definitely overstated, until I started to look at my own life and the things that were more important to me than God. I discovered a major problem with my need for security. Does my need for security usurp energy and devotion that really belongs to God?

If we accept this view of addiction, we are all addicted. To engage in the process of human life is to be addicted, because we all move our worship from God to other things.

Romans 7 is a powerful description of dynamics similar to a person's struggle with addiction. Note the powerful struggle to be free and how difficult it is for Paul. "But in fact it is no longer I that do it, but sin that dwells within me" (v. 17). "For I do not do the good I want, but the evil I do not want is what I do" (v. 19).

Any who struggles with a serious addiction know this feeling intimately. Repeatedly they decide that they will stop the addiction. Repeatedly they fall back. Think of smokers you have known and how often they try to stop before they are successful. Sometimes the resolve lasts only until the time for the next cigarette. Alcoholics resolve to stop drinking, but time and again they "fall off the wagon." Persons addicted to gossip resolve to be done with gossip, but before they know it they are at it again. This is because each addiction is a habit with a drive supporting it.

As one tries to stop, pressure builds until the person gives in again. There is momentary comfort when engaging in the addictive behavior. Then the guilt sets in, setting the scene for the next attempt at control and the next failure.

In this passage the apostle Paul notes that he "delights in the law of God" but is enslaved to another law (v. 22-23).

Addiction, then, is the prototype of the human condition—knowing where we should be and where we want to be, but feeling powerless in achieving it. Like Paul, we long for deliverance.

There is a wonderful poem by John Donne that speaks to the desire for deliverance.

> Batter my heart, three person'd God; for you
> As yet but knock, breathe, shine, and seek to mend;
> That I may rise and stand, o'erthrow me and bend
> Your force, to break, blow, burn, and make me new.
> I, like an usurp'd town, t'another due,
> Labor to admit you, but oh, to no end;
> Reason, your viceroy in me, me should defend,
> But is captiv'd, and proves weak or untrue.
> Yet dearly I love you, and would be loved fain,
> But am betroth'd unto your enemy:

Divorce me, untie, or break that knot again,
Take me to you, imprison me, for I,
Except you enthral me, never shall be free,
Nor ever chaste, except you ravish me.

The question then becomes how God breaks through as both Paul and John Donne and countless others have wondered.

Two separate sources point us in the same direction. First, the solution to the predicament in Romans 7 is found in the first verses of chapter 8 (1-3). In this passage there is the sense that the solution lies beyond human power. While will is important, so often even with a will to change it just doesn't happen. The implication of this passage is that there is a force outside our will which may need to be added to it to give strength for the task.

The second clue about how to end an addiction is found in steps two and three of the Alcoholics Anonymous Twelve Steps, the steps all AA members take on their pathway to sobriety. All of the twelve steps are instructive.

In recent years a wide range of other Twelve Step programs have been started for dealing with other addictions. While Twelve Step programs may not be for everyone, these programs are still the most effective self-help movements in existence, possibly because of the spiritual focus and the power of being in community.

Steps two and three of the Twelve Step program say,

2. Came to believe that a power greater than ourselves could restore us to sanity.
3. Made a decision to turn our will and our lives over to the care of God as we understood him.

A major emphasis in the Twelve Step program is that

denial is not permitted. Jerry's need to speak to the church, and his confession, were central to his recovery.

This takes us to the final point as we look at the spiritual issues related to addiction. To gain victory over addiction we depend on grace, a point made strongly by Gerald May. This is a difficult concept, because we feel that we should be able to deal with our addictions alone and in our own power.

Some people who are successful in quitting their addictive behavior can't explain why it worked this time, when it failed at other times. They just "knew" that this was it.

The point is that the addict must continue trying. The Christian has an added support, God's grace. "My grace is sufficient for you" (2 Cor. 12:9).

At the beginning of this section we asked the question whether addiction is a spiritual issue or a disease. There is no doubt that it is both a spiritual issue and a disease.

Treatment

Treatment will vary, depending on the addiction. Providing help for persons with addictions to substances may be the easiest, since there are a variety of organizations and groups, such as those mentioned above, where people are trained to work with addicted persons.

The more difficult treatments, and the more painful for Christians, are treatments for persons addicted to power, sex drives, abusive behaviors, and religion. Sexual abuse, for example, has little to do with sex. It has to do with power, whether it is in a congregation, the home, counseling setting, or on the streets. We are only beginning to come out of our denial and face the fact that these addictive behaviors occur in each congregation and in a good percentage of Christian homes.

Within the church, addicted people often hide their addiction. This may be because churches have often looked on addiction simplistically as sin and not illness. The church has often seen the addicted person as different from the other "good" people in the congregation. The person with the problem is shunned.

Another reason for not dealing with addictions is the perceived mission of the church. Discussion generally centers on evangelism or social concerns, thus not dealing with the struggles all persons experience in life.

Some of the later questions focus on the church's role. This is also dealt with in the last chapter of the book.

Walking alongside each other may be the most effective ministry we can provide anyone—in the name of Christ.

For Further Study

1. Think back to the chapter on life stages. How might addictions develop at different ages and stages of life?

2. Who are the enablers of addictions? What makes them enablers? If you are studying this in a group and someone in the group has had to face enabling an addictive behavior, have the person share her/his process in dealing with this.

3. Think about Bible stories you know. Identify persons that may have been addicted to substances or drives. Read those stories. How were the persons confronted? What was their response? What was God's (Christ's) role? What is the good news in these situations?

4. Describe the fears of persons in the faith community in dealing with addictions and persons involved. How might your congregation respond to a "Jerry" in your midst?

5. During the past several years, the Christian community has had to confront the issues surrounding clergy

abuse of vulnerable persons in their congregations, institutions, and broader denominational settings. How does the discussion of addictions apply here?

6. Think about ways codependency exists in the church. In what ways do the teachings of the church support codependency? What teachings would make it difficult for a codependent to question or confront the addicted person?

7. What connections are there between addictions and the biological-physical-social-spiritual functioning of a person? (Discussion from chapter 3)

8. Arterburn and Felton make the comment that people can be addicted to their religion and not necessarily believe in God. Discuss this statement. Consider the definitions of addiction.

Additional Resources

Anderson, Leith. *A Church for the 21st Century*. Minneapolis: Bethany House Publishers, 1992.

Apthorp, Stephen P. *Alcohol and Substance Abuse: A Clergy Handbook*. Ridgefield: Morehouse-Barlow, 1985.

Arterburn, Stephen and Felton, Jack. *Faith That Hurts; Faith That Heals*. Nashville: Oliver Nelson, 1993.

Hill, Karen, with revisions by Balthazar, Hector. *Helping You Helps Me: A Guide for Self-Help Groups*. Ottawa: Canadian Council on Social Development, 1987.

Keller, John E. *Alcoholics and Their Families: A Guide for Clergy and Congregations*. New York: Harper Collins, 1991.

Madara, Edward J. and Messe, Abigail (eds.). *The Self-Help Sourcebook: Finding and Forming Mutual Aid Self-Help Groups*. New York: St. Clares-Riverside Medical Center, 1990.

May, Gerald. *Addiction and Grace*. San Francisco: Harper & Row, 1988.

Miller, J. Keith. *A Hunger for Healing: The Twelve Steps as a Classic Model for Christian Spiritual Growth*. San Francisco: Harper Collins, 1991.

Shutt, Joyce M. *Steps to Hope: Coping with Dependency and Failure Through the Beatitudes and Twelve-Step Programs*. Scottdale: Herald Press, 1990.

Wuthnow, Robert. *Sharing the Journey: Support Groups and America's New Quest for Community*. New York: The Free Press, 1994.

The Twelve Steps
1. We admit that we are powerless over alcohol—that our lives have become unmanageable.
2. Came to believe that a power greater than ourselves could restore us to sanity.
3. Made a decision to turn our will and our lives over to the care of God as we understood Him.
4. Made a searching and serious oral inventory of ourselves.
5. Admitted to God, to ourselves, and to another human being the exact nature of our wrongs.
6. Were entirely ready to have God remove all these defects of character.
7. Humbly ask him to remove our shortcomings.
8. Made a list of all persons we have harmed, and became willing to make amends to them all.
9. Made direct amends to such people wherever possible, except when to do so would injure them or others.
10. Continued to take personal inventory and, when we were wrong, promptly admitted it.
11. Sought through prayer and meditation to improve our conscious contact with God as we understand Him, praying only for knowledge of His will for us and the power to carry that out.
12. Having had a spiritual awakening as the result of these

steps, we tried to carry this message to alcoholics and to practice these principles in all our affairs.

9

Shattered Dreams

Scripture
Luke 8:26-39

Opening Thoughts

Scripture does not contain examples of schizophrenia. Possibly the closest we come in the Bible to a description of a psychotic mental illness is the story of the casting out of the demons from the man who lived in the tombs into the herd of pigs (Luke 8:26-39). In fact, Scripture speaks of "spirits" and demons instead of mental illness. (Refer to the discussion of this issue in chapter four.)

It is possible that a number of these people suffered from what we now know as schizophrenia. While we do not have strong biblical examples of schizophrenia, it is still important that we discuss the shattered dreams in the midst of the congregation that come from the illness we know as schizophrenia.

If we were to ask someone not familiar with mental illness to describe a person with such an illness, in all likelihood the description would be somewhat different from most of the people we have considered thus far in this book. Likely someone with bizarre thoughts, delusions, hallucinations, and disturbed behavior would be described. Our respondent might remember movies like *One Flew Over the Cuckoo's Nest*, which describes life in a particularly oppressive mental hospital. Or the person might remember books written by people diagnosed as suffering from schizophrenia, like *I Never Promised You a Rose Garden*. In this story Hannah Green describes, in great detail, her inner experience during her course of treatment for schizophrenia.

In whatever way persons with psychotic conditions are described, it would be dramatic. It would also be tinged with fear, for if there is one thing we humans fear, it is the possibility that we could "lose our minds."

But are psychotic conditions the way we imagine them? Do we need to fear them? Like all things, once we start to understand them fear decreases. Fears are largely based on the unknown. We begin to see people who struggle with these difficult disorders in a different light. We see them as people first. Only later do we see their disorders.

These disorders are made worse by stigma (addressed in the next chapter), including stigma expressed by Christians. For this reason, a chapter on these severe mental conditions is necessary.

Story One

Matt is thirty. He lives in subsidized housing in downtown Vancouver. In fact, he does not really live in a house. He lives in an old hotel, where a number of other people with schizophrenia live, each in their own rooms. Typically his day begins about noon, when he rouses himself from bed. Often he will lie for hours wondering whether he should get up or not. He can't seem to find the motivation even to rouse himself.

His daily routine goes something like this: he gets

dressed, often forgetting to tend to the usual hygiene, like brushing his teeth or combing his hair. He leaves his room and begins slowly to wander the streets. He stops to speak to a friend, but the conversation does not go much beyond "Hi." Then there is more wandering.

By 5:00 p.m. he stops at a street mission, where occasionally he gets supper. Sometimes he cooks for himself or buys himself a hamburger. But it is the end of the month and his welfare check is spent. After supper he goes back to his room because he is afraid of being out at night. He listens to the radio, or often just sits in the dark by himself until two or three a.m. Then it is time for bed, and the cycle repeats itself.

It was not always this way. Matt remembers when he was in high school. He was a good student, getting top grades. He had friends. Then, in first year university, it all started to change. He noted trouble concentrating. Marks began to drop.

A couple of months later he began hearing voices, commenting about him. In fact he felt that the radio and television were speaking directly to him, telling him what to do. He went to the student health services and was sent directly to the hospital. He got better with treatment, but found reentry into the community difficult.

It was not possible to return to studies, and he could not find the energy to get a job. The desire to be normal was so great that he stopped taking his medication and his condition began to deteriorate. He has been admitted to the hospital five times now. But when he is discharged, he does not keep his appointments with the mental health team.

It seems he just can't organize himself enough to keep his appointment every two weeks for an injection of medication that will prevent a relapse. Besides, he often feels better off medication, until he gets too sick to remain out of hospital.

Matt's family lives in another city. Aside from a few phone calls and a visit every few years, there is little contact. Family members worry about Matt, but feel helpless to bring about change in his life. This leaves them with a deep, almost constant pain.

Story Two

Melanie, twenty-four, first had psychotic thoughts when she was in high school. Concentration was as difficult for her as for Matt. She also started to hear voices talking about her, developed ideas that people were trying to poison her, and at times felt they were following her. Being in crowds increased her anxiety to the point that she preferred to be alone.

Melanie's parents insisted she see the family doctor, who arranged a consultation with the psychiatrist. She was admitted to the hospital for one month, during which time she learned about her illness, received support, and was established on medication.

Her family remained involved with her and supportive. As her thoughts cleared she returned to school and finished high school. She displayed talent as an artist and was encouraged to attend a college of art.

She paints now. While she has not yet found a market for her art, she has sold an occasional painting. There is a surreal intensity about the paintings that is at once appealing and just a little disturbing.

Occasionally Melanie has feelings of paranoia, but the voices only returned once, briefly. She sees her friends fairly frequently and attends church. While she does not get involved in church, attending is important to her.

People in the congregation show an interest in her. They have been a strong support to her and her family throughout the illness. One of the people who is most supportive indicated that he had a brother diagnosed with schizophrenia some years ago. He knew it was hard for the family and for her, but he, with others, were there to support Melanie and her family.

Focus

This chapter began with two stories because there is such variability in schizophrenia, ranging from those with a poor outcome, like Matt, to people with a moderately good outcome like Melanie. In fact, there is so much variability that schizophrenia is often seen as a group of diseases.

However, not just people who have schizophrenia become psychotic. Others become psychotic for brief periods, up to a month or so, in response to a stress such as a physical illness, drugs, or an event in their life journey.

Still others are ill for a longer time and appear to have schizophrenia, but it disappears in six months, never to return. These people are said to have a schizophreniform psychosis.

In this chapter we will focus on two things. First we will consider what it means to be psychotic. This is important, because some Christians are mistakenly concerned that psychotic conditions like schizophrenia may result from demon possession.

Second, we will consider schizophrenia itself, particularly to raise the question of how we as the church respond to people or their families in the face of this difficult, chronic illness. This support and caring is discussed further in chapter ten.

Search

What Is a Psychosis?

The term *psychotic* has been used a number of times by now without definition. It may be inferred that psychosis has something to do with whether a person has delusions or hallucinations.

To be psychotic is to have a condition in which one is not able to experience reality as others do. Cues from the environment are misinterpreted. Individuals may even have false sensory experiences, known as hallucinations. While commonly hallucinations are heard as voices, they could include seeing things and experiencing strange smells or strange body sensations. In addition the person may have difficulty holding thoughts in order.

A major difficulty is experienced in testing reality. What do we mean by "testing reality"? We all test reality all the time. We may be walking down the street and see someone looking at us. If we do not know the person, we likely ignore the look, reasoning that the person was not looking at us for any particular reason. Or we may hear a faint sound, or think someone called our name. We reason that we must have been mistaken, we must have "heard things."

The person with difficulty in reality testing may not always reason as we do. The person in the crowd may be interpreted as looking that way for a particular reason. The faint sounds become clear hallucinations.

People who experience their world in this altered way try to make sense of their environment by developing an explanation for themselves about what is happening. Their underlying premise is wrong because they have failed in testing reality. Their explanation of what is happening then becomes delusional.

A delusion is defined as a fixed false belief out of keeping with that of others with similar intelligence and religious or cultural background. For example, a person who experiences a psychosis may think that a lot of people are looking at him and even talking about him. To him this means that he must be important. If this conclusion is accompanied by feeling very special, a person may start to feel God relates to her in a special way. The opposite may also occur when a person with feelings of paranoia feels threatened or persecuted by others.

When voices are heard it is not unusual for persons to think it is God speaking to them. From here it is a small step to feeling that they have been given a special mission from God to save the world. Thus the total psychotic experience gets explained by a delusion. This is very different from Christians who may note that God speaks to them but quickly acknowledge that they do not hear God's voice audibly.

People with a psychosis often have difficulty with emotions as well. They experience profound feelings of anxiety, sadness, anger, or even peace or specialness. Because they have difficulty analyzing or understanding the emotion, these too become part of the delusions.

When Christians search for a frame of reference that helps us understand our experience in life, we reach for our faith as the over-riding frame of reference. Many people who become psychotic do the same thing, reaching for God and their own understanding of the battle between good and evil as a framework in which to place or explain their new experiences. Because their reality testing is impaired, and because their experiences are so far from what others experience, the delusions they form seem strange to us.

It is tempting to try to correct the beliefs of someone going through a psychotic experience. Usually this is not possible, as the beliefs are held firmly, rooted in that person's reality. As persons come out of psychosis, either spontaneously or as the result of treatment, they develop insight and leave the ideas on their own.

It is common, in my work with Christians who have become psychotic, to discover that numerous attempts have been made by well-meaning Christian lay people and some ministers to diagnose these people as suffering from evil spirits or demons. Many have had prayers for deliverance with no definable benefit. In fact, these experiences have sometimes been incorporated by the patient into the psychotic experience. My plea is that, if deliverance in the sense of dealing with evil spirits is to be considered, that there first be a solid psychiatric consultation, for the person may be suffering from a psychotic disorder.

Schizophrenia

Schizophrenia is the most common of the psychotic disorders, affecting up to one percent of the population. Many people who do not understand the disease assume that it produces a split personality, whatever that means to them. In fact, schizophrenia is not that at all. It is a disease of thought, perceptions, and emotion that occurs in a mild or severe form. It appears most commonly in adolescence or early adulthood and in many persons persists through life.

It has been noted that up to 25 percent of people with schizophrenia have a good outcome. Another 50 percent will have a number of relapses. Only 25 percent will be so severely affected that their condition will continue to deteriorate.

While the symptoms will not be discussed in detail, it is important that we understand that the symptoms of schizophrenia are divided into two groups.

The first are called the *positive* symptoms. These are the symptoms of the psychotic disorders we have just discussed. We tend to focus on them because they are so dramatic. These symptoms, however, are also the most responsive to treatment. Most disappear over time with the proper medication. Such symptoms are most common at the beginning of the illness and may recur at different times throughout the illness but for the most part are highly treatable.

The second group of symptoms are called the *negative* symptoms. These include lack of energy, lack of drive, isolation from others, loss of sustained interest in anything, and a blunting of emotion. These symptoms give the person more difficulty than the positive ones because without energy, drive, and sustained interest it is very hard to get going with life.

Commonly the family of the person diagnosed as having schizophrenia in early adulthood or late adolescence is the first to notice that something is wrong. Often the first signs are that their son or daughter is having trouble concentrating and is losing interest in school. The person with schizophrenia may start to withdraw from friends.

This early stage could last for six or more months before positive symptoms are noted. Until these symptoms are observed it is hard to know what is happening. Often this period is viewed as just problems in adjusting to the tasks of young adulthood. The positive symptoms usually bring the person to treatment.

As the person responds to treatment and there is no longer any sign of psychosis, it appears to the family that their son or daughter has been returned to them. However, the battle is only half over, because now they note that their family member is tired, lacks drive, and just can't seem to get themselves going. It is hard not to have expectations that they will just pick up the lives they had before this all started. After all, their son or daughter "looks normal." He or she just appears unmotivated. They reason that all would be well if their child would only try harder.

Persons recovering from the psychosis want to get going. They just can't. They may not be able to put into words that they just don't have the drive or energy to reestablish their former lives. They may have trouble concentrating or being able to read complex material. It all demands effort which is beyond them.

A courageous young woman describes her struggle with schizophrenia.

Schizophrenia

Once you were a glowing, brilliant star
Shining, twinkling, sparkling.
Anticipating bright years to come,
A future strong and blazing.

But just as you were about to reach your prime
A time of fresh beginning,
Your light suddenly lost its precious glow,
And quickly began its dimming.

As other stars all around you shone,
You watched them as their life moved on.
You couldn't move and you couldn't shine
And wondered where your light had gone.

And the others laughed and lived and loved,
With energy, drive, and desire.
They became polished and glossy,
While you lost your last bit of fire.

And in the darkness you just existed,
Living in a black, gloomy state.
While other stars tried to reflect their light,
To prevent your impending fate.

Once you were a glowing, brilliant star
But were lost when life was best.

> Now you have passed your youthful days
> And have awoken to your death.
> > —Heather Penner (used by permission)

Other patients cry, telling me how they wished they could do more, and that they felt useless. They compare themselves with others, their family, and friends. They have difficulty accepting that it is hard for them to accomplish just the normal tasks anyone would do in living. It is hard for the friends and family as well. It is easy to see their loved one as not trying, being lazy, or just giving up.

There may be a particular problem for people in the church, because so often we have expectations that all a person has to do is try, or all we have to do is pray, and it will be all right. If we were to name this stage of the illness, it would best be called the stage of frustration.

Some people spontaneously get better over the course of a few years. More likely, improvement is slow, often interrupted by relapses. Medication helps, but most people with schizophrenia don't want to be on medication. Yet they find that it is often the only way they can function.

Until recently the medication that was available worked much better on the positive symptoms, keeping the psychotic thoughts and behavior in check, rather than on the negative symptoms. We are, however, beginning to see the first medications that provide more help with the negative symptoms.

What Causes Schizophrenia?

The last years have been productive in understanding the cause of schizophrenia. When I started in psychiatry, one of the theories about schizophrenia was that it was caused by bad parenting.

Other theorists have suggested that schizophrenia arises from trying to live in a crazy society. In the same vein, some Christians have believed that the psychotic features of schizophrenia arise out of evil spirits or demon possession. I believe we can state that all these ideas of causes of schizophrenia are wrong.

We have known for some time that schizophrenia has a genetic base. Identical twins will share the disease only 40 percent of the time, while siblings share it 8 percent of the time. This means that schizophrenia is inherited at a low rate but still has a genetic base. Other factors, including psychological and social ones, may be the stressors that precipitate the onset of the disease.

A recent discovery is that people with schizophrenia use less glucose and have less blood flow to the frontal lobes of the brain. Their ventricles (spaces in the center of the brain) are larger than in people without schizophrenia.

We also know that schizophrenia is a disease of at least one of the chemicals in the brain (dopamine) and that the effective medications work to help correct that imbalance. So it is clear that schizophrenia is intertwined with biology.

Schizophrenia and the Church

Why have we devoted a whole chapter to psychotic conditions in a study about mental health and Christianity? While these disorders are common, they are not nearly as common as depression and anxiety. Many of us may never know someone with the disorder.

We have devoted space to them because they are so poorly understood within and outside the church. As was mentioned earlier, in the church we have difficulty with people who may have strange beliefs about the faith. We may speak of how God communicates with and even "speaks" to us, but we don't hear the voice.

For us to have someone claim to actually hear God sounds strange. It is beyond the experience of most of us.

We might think it a particularly important religious experience except that it is accompanied by other signs of psychosis. The mixture of the psychotic with the religious is intensely uncomfortable for us.

As members of society, we tend to participate in the stigma that people suffering from schizophrenia feel. We tend to be a little afraid of anyone labeled as psychotic. I have resisted using the word until now, but we often refer to them as "crazy." In fact, our society is full of stories and jokes about crazy people. In movies they are often portrayed as dangerous—for example, psychotic killers. Or they are portrayed as clowns, as in the movie *Crazy People*. They are seldom portrayed as people who live quiet lives, love and are loved, may work, and have normal feelings. They are seldom portrayed as one of us. And yet they are.

Few are dangerous, in fact danger is found in people without schizophrenia in almost the same frequency. Occasionally a person with schizophrenia may be dangerous as a result of delusions, but this is rare.

They too may despair and become suicidal. Either of these situations are indications for immediate help, usually in the hospital. The more usual situation is described by a nurse I worked with who was trying to describe a new patient to me. Struggling to convey what she meant, she smiled and said, "You know, he has that wonderful gentleness that so many with schizophrenia have."

Few people with schizophrenia remain psychotic. However, many struggle with the negative symptoms. They tend to live lonely, somewhat frustrating lives, wishing to be productive but finding they can't. In this process their self-esteem suffers a great deal. Yet almost systematically they are excluded. They don't push themselves forward, and mostly we don't care enough to seek them out.

The families of persons with serious problems need a support system. How do we stand by the family in the early stages of the illness when they struggle to get their loved one help, when they feel fear, frustration, and often failure? The initial period can be very trying. However, after the early period there is another, more difficult task—providing long-term support for the family.

Our second story tells how a Christian stood by Melanie and her family, because he understood. His brother had experienced the same illness. I know from conversations with Melanie's family that this was the most helpful contact they had throughout their ordeal. They felt there was someone who understood to help guide them through it.

The norm in Western society is based on people being productive. We feel good when we can work. We like to earn our keep. Our self-esteem depends on it. Plus the Protestant work ethic dictates that whoever doesn't work shouldn't eat. "Doing" determines worth.

However, persons with schizophrenia often cannot find work. They may not be as punctual as others or able to work as fast and as long as others. Therefore they often cannot find employment in our competitive workplaces.

Treating a mental illness, finding a room, and possibly covering living expenses may be very expensive for the family. Are there ways we can help? And what about the individual with the disorder? A young man with the disease told me that for four days in one week he had not had anything to eat because he had run out of money.

Conclusion

As you will have noted, schizophrenia is a complex disease that affects almost every area of life, both for the person with the disorder and for the family.

Other chronic health problems carry similar weights. Christians have a responsibility to respond to those with major mental difficulties, both in and outside the church. In the last chapter we will look at this response in greater detail.

For Further Study

1. What is generally understood by "losing one's mind"? How has that perception changed through the discussion in this chapter?

2. From where do Christians draw the connection between demon possession and mental illness? Is it still common today? Discuss.

3. How has your perception of schizophrenia changed when the possibility of a biological base is introduced? Does this affect how we view people with this disease?

4. Consider the man in the tombs. Should this man be considered psychotic? Demon possessed? Both? If possible, check various commentaries that discuss this passage. How does this change your view of what happened in that incident?

5. What are the implications for the church? Do we help correct false impressions shared by many in society? Most people now live in the community, since few patients are still housed in mental hospitals. How do we respond to them when they are living near us? How do we welcome them, support them? What does the gospel have to say to the church on this issue? In what ways might Hebrews 13:1-3,16 apply to Christians' relationship to persons with psychotic disorders?

6. Discuss the faith and civic communities' challenges in meeting the needs of the person with schizophrenia, since patients are rarely kept in mental hospitals.

7. If a member of your family has been diagnosed with a psychotic disorder, what kind of support/help do you need?

8. Define "work," "self-esteem," "doing," "being" in terms of the dominant theology in your faith community. What is the biblical basis for that view? In what ways is that view absorbed through the dominant culture where you grew up and live presently?

9. A young woman with schizophrenia attended a healing service in which she received prayer. She responded with an improvement in her condition. She still had symptoms of schizophrenia but now required less medication and had a greater degree of stability. Was she at least partly healed? Did Christ respond to her as to the man among the tombs?

10. Think about your community. What work options and opportunities are there for long-term mentally ill persons? What opportunities could be created?

Additional Resources

Fowler, Ruth. *A Stranger in Our Midst: A Congregational Study on Prolonged Mental Illness*. St. Louis: Pathways to Promise, 1988.

Green, Hannah. *I Never Promised You a Rose Garden*. New York: Signet, 1964.

Hinckley, Jack and JoAnn. *Breaking Points*. Grand Rapids: Zondervan, 1985.

Oates, Wayne E. *The Religious Care of the Psychiatric Patient*. Louisville: Westminster Press, 1978.

Occasional Papers No. 11. *Essays on Spiritual Bondage and Deliverance*. Elkhart: Associated Mennonite Biblical Seminaries, 1989.

Shifrin, Jennifer. *Pathways to Partnership: An Awareness & Resource Guide on Mental Illness*. St. Louis: Pathways to Promise, 1989.

Torrey, E. Fuller. *Surviving Schizophrenia: A Family Manual* (rev. ed.) San Francisco: Harper & Row, 1988.

Walsh, Maryellen. *Schizophrenia: Straight Talk for Family & Friends*. New York: Warner Books, 1985.

Videos:
*Shattered Dreams. National Film Board of Canada. Twenty-eight minutes.
No Place to Go. National Film Board of Canada. Twenty-eight minutes.

*This film inspired the title of this chapter.

10

Whatever You Do . . .

Scripture
Matthew 25:31-46; Matthew 5:13-16

Opening Thoughts

In this chapter we deal with the "so what?" aspect of the book. You will note at the end of the chapter that there are two options For Further Study (A and B). Look at the options provided and decide how you and/or your group would like to respond to the content of this book. You might want to follow the pattern set in previous chapters. Or you might want to let the creative juices flow and use suggestions from For Further Study (B).

In this book we have considered mental health problems from the mild to the severe. A subtheme in most chapters has been how these problems are encountered in the church. In this chapter we will discuss stigma, the isolation of people who have problems, and how we express our love for them individually and as a church.

Story

Bonnie was different. She was likely the poorest girl in our class in school. She didn't dress as well as the others. It was said that she didn't smell nice and often looked dirty. Her marks weren't good. We knew she would drop out of school as soon as she could. She sat in isolation at the back of the class.

I was a young fellow from the right side of the tracks. We certainly were not poor. My hygiene was good. My marks were passable. However, I was terribly insecure. I had few friends and felt it keenly. I wished desperately to be accepted, to be like my classmates who seemed to have it all together.

One day it dawned on me. If I could show just how much I disliked Bonnie and what she represented, then I would be like the others and they would accept me. I started a campaign of teasing and ridiculing Bonnie in front of my classmates every chance I got. The others would laugh and it would spur me on to greater ridicule.

One day, while teasing Bonnie, the unexpected happened. Bonnie, who until now had been dry-eyed, holding her head high, started to cry! She looked at me through her tears and asked, "Why are you doing this to me?"

I was amazed that Bonnie would cry. I had never considered that possibility! I hadn't thought she would have feelings. That night I didn't sleep. Bonnie's tears and her question haunted me. I knew I had no option but to ask her forgiveness. And I knew it would have to be in front of my classmates.

Focus

The story of Bonnie is not really a story about the mental health problems we have discussed in this book. However, it has profound implications for mental health. It carries the theme of being isolated because one is different, either because of feeling a failure, or because there is something visibly different.

Bonnie was isolating herself by staying alone, but likely she had no choice. Groups isolate and exclude those they feel to be different, and my classmates had certainly done that to Bonnie.

Finally the story of Bonnie is an example of how it is possible to dehumanize other persons, to consider them so different and so inferior that we don't attribute to them the qualities of "popular" persons. This is the basis for stigma.

Search

Stigma is a prejudicial attitude toward another person or group of people, class, or race because of their origin, attributes, or condition. We all participate in stigmatizing to a greater or lesser extent. We contribute to stigma whenever we judge persons or their capabilities because of their race, their socioeconomic status, their disabilities, their beliefs, or their appearance.

We also stigmatize by applying labels. People stigmatize by labeling others "non-Christians," "conservatives," "liberals"—as if they are in a totally different class. Giving persons labels seems to give one the group's authority to exclude the labeled persons without reference to who they are as people.

People with mental problems are often stigmatized. People with a more visible problem, like the person who is obviously hallucinating or has strange behavior, may be stigmatized as being mentally ill. People with milder forms of difficulty, like depression or anxiety problems, may be stigmatized as not trying hard enough or not being right with God. The person who responds to people with problems in this way does not see them as individuals, each with their own unique needs, but categorizes them in a way that diminishes them as human beings.

Stigmatized people live on the margins of society or on the margins of their social group. They may try to hide their disorder because they fear the reactions to them. As a result of stigma, they may be subject to attitudes that say they should not be in society. They may not find work or good accommodation. They may receive less money with which to live. They often are more open to judgment or exclusion from the group.

Stigma is born out of ignorance and fear. It is also born out of our own sense of insecurity when we wish to remain comfortable in the world we have structured for ourselves.

But what if we were visibly different? Or what if we were struggling through divorce? Were homosexual? Were a teenager who was pregnant? What about persons existing in their own private hell of depression or anxiety? Are our churches places where we are open to others?

Mental Health Services and the Community

People with mental illness in our society have been stigmatized over the centuries. Large hospitals for the mentally ill—that are more like human warehouses than hospitals—still exist in many parts of the world. However, many hospitals have improved. There has been great emphasis on reducing the number of people in the hospitals as a result of the process of deinstitutionalization.

People with mental problems are now usually treated in general hospitals, in community centers, or in church-related mental health programs or hospitals. This shift of care from hospital to community has been only partly successful, because often persons' needs are not met adequately when they are in the community, just as they may not have been met adequately in the large mental hospitals.

In large North American cities we now have a problem with homeless or street people, who exist on the street for lack of care and finances. Many of these people have mental disorders.

This shift in focus to the community opens service opportunities for the church. However, to develop these opportunities, the church will first have to consider carefully its call to work with the ill, the downtrodden, and people who have expended their limited resources.

Christ and Stigma

We can look to the life of Christ to understand the Christian approach to the problem of stigma. The Gospels record how Christ ate with tax collectors, some of the most despised people in the Jewish society of his day. He associated closely with women, including a prostitute, which was out of keeping with the stigma in the society of his day.

As the Scripture passage for this chapter we selected Matthew 25, the parable of the sheep and the goats. Note Christ's stance in identifying with the poor, the sick, the hungry, the thirsty, and those in prison. This chapter suggests a full identification with the people not accepted elsewhere in society.

In fact, Christ goes further than this. He notes that "just as you did it to one of the least of these who are members of my family, you did it to me" (Matt. 25:40). This suggests that being there for those in need is service for Christ. In whatever way caring is expressed, it requires crossing the boundaries of stigma.

For years I have read the parable of the sheep and the goats without realizing the incredible secret of the parable. I had always read it to mean what we have just discussed

—service to someone else in the name of Christ. Then I began to see that the parable had an additional meaning. It deals with the incarnation of Christ in those who are poor, hungry, thirsty, sick, naked, or in prison. If we could only see the person in need as Christ embodied, how would this change our attitude to the people we see who are stigmatized by both society and the church?

The embodiment of Christ in those in need changes our perspective dramatically. When Bonnie looked at me and through tears asked, "Why are you doing this to me?" it was not just Bonnie asking the question, but Christ.

This is only half the story. Christ also lives in the person who responds to the need. A few years ago I attended church when I was in deep personal need. I had just had a major setback at work and was doubting myself professionally and as a person. As we started to sing, I started to cry. Soon I was sobbing.

I felt embarrassed but could not stop the tears. I was far too near the front to walk out gracefully to compose myself. After all, people would notice and wonder what was happening. In the middle of my pain, suddenly I felt arms around me, hugging me, holding me tight. It was my sixteen-year-old daughter who had recognized my pain, moved over, and now was holding me. She hugged me as I sobbed. I am eternally grateful to Jennifer for that act of kindness, particularly coming from an adolescent who might be expected to hide in embarrassment.

However, the act of kindness has grown in significance for me, for in Jen's love I also felt the arms of Christ holding me and caring for me.

Some years ago I was doing a study in a mental hospital on a Caribbean island. My study often took me to the locked ward which, in tropical style, was built around an open quadrangle. It was entered through a barred gate.

When the patients saw me coming, they would crowd

around the gate. The nurse would push and prod them to clear a path for me. They bombarded me with questions. "Can I go home?" "Won't you let me out?"

There was nothing I could do. They weren't my patients. I didn't even know who they were. I felt so helpless that I hated going there. Then I decided to do something different. I began to touch them, each one. Throwing my arm around one, shaking the other's hand, I tried to have a comment for each. They crowded me even more, but now I enjoyed it as some eagerly told me about themselves or asked questions about me.

In those few moments we became a community. They stopped being this crowding, demanding group of mental patients and became instead, if only for a moment, a community of friends. I knew that these few moments were likely inconsequential in their long-term treatment, but what was the low point of my day became the highlight. Could it be that in each I was encountering Christ?

The Church as a Hospital

If the church is the place for hurting people, possibly we need to consider its function as a hospital. To be a hospital implies that persons are sick and accepted as such. It is also recognized that the goal of being in the hospital is to provide care leading to cure, healing, or palliation.

Often I have heard people who are depressed, anxious, or going through a family crisis tell me that the church is the last place they would go for support, because they are afraid they will be judged. They see the church as a place where people come to worship and be happy. It is not for people like them with problems. Some have been to the church, and they tell me how they were hurt either by being ignored when they dared not reach out themselves, or feeling judged or isolated if they did speak about their problems.

If the church is to be a hospital, it will discover that the Christ in a pure white robe is really just a Sunday school picture. The Christ of the road met people in the effort and the dirt and grime of life.

Being a hospital is costly. However, if this is the calling of the church, then it must prepare for it by equipping its members with skills for helping others. Resources will be required to help members know how to understand people, how truly to be with them, and how to recognize the need for more expert help when necessary.

This means that churches interested in being hospitals for people in pain will need to examine themselves to know where they participate in stigmatizing others. This will affect educational and other support programs for individuals and groups in the congregation.

There is, however, a problem with the model of the church as a hospital. A hospital suggests a distinction between staff and patients. Staff are there to serve patients who have needs. If the church adopts the hospital model and applies the hospital tradition to its organization, it cannot be effective. If we look at ourselves honestly, we see that we are all in need. The church cannot afford distinctions.

A small book entitled *The Wounded Healer*, by Henri Nouwen (1988), has been a great help for people who want to serve others. Nouwen notes that our strength as healers arises from recognizing our own wounds. In recognizing our own brokenness, we are able to empathize with people. That gives us compassion for them, and allows us to love them in the depth of their pain.

In another book, *The Road to Daybreak*, Nouwen (1979) describes how the L'Arche Community, composed of people with severe developmental disabilities, embodies love. These persons, together with their friends, have shown him Christ and have ministered to him despite and often through their own limitations. We cannot help others without realizing that we have been helped by them.

The Church as Community

So we come to the final model of the church that seeks to be there for people with difficulties of whatever sort. In this model we become a community where we worship, pray, learn, help, and are helped—all together. Achieving community in an individualistic society is very difficult.

The model of community is the model of the church in Scripture. If the church is to be a community, all experiencing problems, pain, or mental disorders must be included. Just being together does not make us a community but merely a group of people. Christ defined community as a place where we "love one another. Just as I have loved you, you also should love one another. By this everyone will know that you are my disciples, if you have love for one another" (John 13:34-35).

If we accept the command to love one another as a basis for community, we must realize that this takes time and commitment. Scott Peck (1988), in *The Different Drum,* characterizes the steps in forming community. The first stage is *pseudo-community*. In this stage we like being together and it feels good. But we don't address the hard questions because we cannot risk losing our good feeling. We can't include others because we would become uncomfortable.

The second stage is *chaos.* Our pseudo-community does not meet our need any longer. It is too superficial. We are dying for lack of human contact, because we want and need more than handshakes, platitudes, and the isolation that makes us hide who we are.

If we persist through chaos we enter the next stage—*death*. Peck compares this stage to Christ's resignation to death in his struggle in the garden.

Here we give up the struggle. Something new and wonderful happens in this stage. We become aware of our great need to love and to be loved. This realization allows us to give up our own agendas, in a sense to "die to self." Then we seek together for ways to express Christ's love to everyone. This ushers in the final phase.

In the stage of *community* we learn to love others, care for those in pain and share their pain, whether they are inside or outside our church. We are open to differences. Love is expressed, not because persons "fit in," but because of who each is and the way we are as Christ to each other.

Some Practical Suggestions

There is a temptation to end this chapter with the lofty sentiments just expressed. However, a number of you may be saying, "That's fine. But now what do we do?"

Let's look at this question from the perspective of what we can do as individuals, as a group, as a church, and as a group of churches. Robert Wuthnow (1994) provides excellent insights into the roles and ministries of support groups in the congregational setting. This book is highly recommended as a basis in the planning stages for ministries in small groups.

The Individual

The individual level can be illustrated by a story.

Jesus gave us a new light on a variety of subjects—a new way of seeing, much like the story of an old man walking down the beach at dawn, who noticed a young man ahead of him picking up starfish and flinging them into the sea. Catching up with the youth, the older man asked what he was doing. The young man answered that the stranded starfish would die if left until the morning sun.

"But the beach goes on for miles, and there are millions

of starfish," countered the old man. "How can your effort make any difference?"

The young man looked at the starfish in his hand, then threw it to safety in the waves. "It makes a difference to this one," he said (from *Clergy Pak*, Week 1, July 2, 1989, The Whole People of God, C 4-4).

Here are ways we can as individuals interact with mental health needs.

1. Being open to people will greatly depend on how we recognize and deal with our own hurts, needs, and problems and willingness to let others help us.

2. We must know ourselves. We can't help everyone. There are times when our gifts, abilities, and education are not suitable for helping persons with some of the problems and illnesses discussed in this book. We need to be honest with ourselves, take an inventory of our gifts and skills, and be willing to refer persons for professional help.

3. We need to be knowledgeable about the challenges and problems in relating to persons with mental diseases. This book is a small step in that direction. Each community has a variety of resources available. While one doesn't need to know everything, it helps to have read enough to understand what another person is going through. For example, if a friend or family member is going through a depression, look for a book or other resource on depression.

4. Speaking with persons responsible for pastoral care may provide insights about how and where one might get involved in the congregation. Sensitivity to the needs of others may also create awareness. A general hint—be quick to listen, slower to speak, and slowest to offer advice. One of the biggest turn-offs is, "If I were you I would. . . ." Remember, a question is often more helpful than a comment.

5. Sharing our own struggles might be the encouragement a hurting person needs—the recognition that he/she is not the only one struggling in life.

6. There are times and circumstances in which all we can be is a friend. Recall (in the chapter on psychotic disorders) the fellow from church who was there for Melanie and her family when it was most needed. Be practical. Often a spontaneous gesture of love will support people through dark times.

7. Confidentiality is vital. What passes between two persons sharing in confidence must remain with the two persons, unless of course there is permission to share the content with someone else. People feel betrayed when confidences, even things that may not be labeled as confidential, become public.

Note the question in the study section as this dimension of caring is processed.

8. Pray. Sometimes all we can do is pray about a situation, especially when trying to deal with the pressures and stresses of being a caregiver.

The Group

1. There is more strength in a group than in an individual for a number of reasons. Groups provide support. They have a wider range of experiences, gifts, knowledge, and skills than an individual. Therefore, explore with a group—fellowship group, Sunday school class, or informal group of interested people—how you as a group can best understand and help persons dealing with the types of mental illnesses mentioned in this book.

2. Belonging to a small group can be one place in which we can share deeply what is going on in our own life. However, it is important that we do not put pressures on a group for dealing with problems that can only be processed adequately by a professionally trained person. A church group can help up to a point—and everyone in the group must be aware of the boundaries.

3. There may be specific needs in your congregation or in your community. A caution here. It is right and good to meet needs. However, it is not appropriate to make another person a project. To be a project is dehumanizing and humiliating. Therefore, motivation in getting involved in ministering to a person with a mental disorder is important. Is it out of love for the person(s) or to fill a "missionary" need?

4. Consider inviting those who appear alone and isolated to your group. Persons with problems tend to isolate themselves and may need to be encouraged to belong to a group that sees the person as well as the illness. There are times, however, when the individual with the illness is more comfortable relating to another individual than to a group.

5. Pray as a group. Allow the vision to form through prayer.

The Church

1. Consider whether your church is interested in serving the specific needs of the congregation for support and caring in a variety of ways, including those who may have problems with their mental health. Create a vision of how this can be done.

2. Consider whether your church has needs for any particular skills, such as how to be a support to others or lay counseling. Do an inventory of your congregational resources. Do resources need to be developed? How can these resources be used?

3. Decide whether your congregation wishes to take on programs for specific needs directly or whether you wish to be a support to those in your congregation already involved in mental health work through their employment or community service. For example, how does your church support those involved in mental-health-related volunteer work in the community? Are their activities seen as part of the mission of your congregation?

4. As was mentioned earlier, there may be labeling and stigmas that need to be processed in a congregation before ministry can begin with persons with mental illnesses.

Our prayer is that churches move to become true communities where individual needs find understanding and support. Then all of us, including those with the specific problems we have discussed in this book, can discover what it means to experience the love of Christ and the power that is there in the faith. The church has a major calling to work for the health and acceptance of all.

For Further Study (A)

1. What does it mean that humans are "created in God's image"? Who is created in God's image? What difference does/should that make when we talk about persons different from the norm in society and church?

2. When does the need for confidentiality become difficult? Have a pastor, lawyer, mental health professional, police officer, or other person help you process this question.

3. What labels or stigmas prevent your congregation from ministering to persons with mental illnesses?

4. In what ways do labels and stigmas come from the surrounding culture? In what ways do they come from religious beliefs?

5. How do you feel about the church being compared to a hospital? Why do you feel that way?

6. Look back at the chapters covered in this book. What threads do you see? What questions remain unanswered? Where are the resources to answer those questions? What questions may never be answered?

7. What practical suggestions would you add to the ones given in this chapter?

8. If you are using this book in a church group, take a look at the organizational structure of the congregation. In what ways does it reflect ministry that is *not* white, middle-class, traditional? How do you feel about that?

9. With what points made in this chapter do you agree/disagree?

10. Moving on—complete the following statements:
As a result of this study I will. . . .
As a result of this study we will. . . .

For Further Study (B)

Considering the variety of needs and mental illnesses described and studied in this book, begin looking at the congregation as a place for meeting those needs. This is a time to dream impossible dreams and let ideas fly. If you're tired of words, here are a few suggestions for thinking about the role of the church. Be innovative! Have fun!

Option 1

Design the ideal congregation

What is your vision?
What is the basis for the vision?
What are your goals?
What are your objectives?
How will you carry out those objectives?
Who will carry them out?
What will help or hinder carrying out those objectives?
What will be considered "success"?

Option 2

Create a worship service or a series of worship services, developing a theme from this book.

Option 3
   Write and present a drama based on this book.

Option 4
   Prepare a multimedia presentation developing some of the main thoughts and concerns in the book.

Option 5
   Create a sculpture or other art form to illustrate a concept of the church's ministry with/to mentally ill persons.

Option 6
   Design your own study as a continuation of the ideas presented in this one, or on any one of the particular topics in the book.

Option 7
   Design a pastoral care program that will meet the needs in your particular congregation.

Resources

Friedman, Edwin H. *Generation to Generation: Family Process in Church & Synagogue*. New York: The Guilford Press, 1985.

Gibble, June A. and Swartz, Fred W., eds. *Called to Caregiving: A Resource for Equipping Deacons in the Believers Church*. Elgin: Brethren Press, 1987.

Govig, Stewart D. *Strong at the Broken Places: Persons with Disabilities and the Church*. Louisville: Westminster/ John Knox Press, 1989.

Haugk, Kenneth C. *Christian Caregiving: A Way of Life*. Augsburg: Fortress Press, 1984.

Lane, Melodee. *Models of Care: For Persons with a Prolonged Mental Illness*. St. Louis: Pathways to Promise, 1988.

Nouwen, Henri. *The Road to Daybreak*. New York: Doubleday, 1988.

_____. *The Wounded Healer*. New York: Dou-
bleday, 1979.

Peck, M. Scott. *The Different Drum*. New York: Simon &
Schuster Trade (Touchstone Books), 1988.

Preheim-Bartel, Dean A. and Neufeldt, Aldred H. *Supportive Care in the Congregation*. Akron: MCC, 1986.

Wuthnow, Robert. *Sharing the Journey: Support Groups and
America's New Quest for Community*. New York: The
Free Press, 1994.

The Authors

 **John Toews** is a professor of psychiatry and the associate dean of continuing medical education at the University of Calgary. He is the author of thirty articles which have appeared in professional journals and is active in a number of professional associations. His areas of interest have been developmental psychiatry, community psychiatry, psychotherapy, and medical education.

Toews graduated from the University of Manitoba with his M.D. degree in 1969, completed his specialty training in psychiatry at the University of Manitoba in 1974, and taught at that university until 1988, when he moved to Calgary.

John has spoken often about and conducted numerous workshops on health and faith for churches, clergy, and university students. This book arises out of insights into relationships between mental health and faith that have emerged from his clinical work and discussing the topic in his speaking and workshop activities.

He and his wife, Johanne, have two children—Paul, age twenty-four and married to Melody; and Jennifer, age twenty-one. They attend the Dalhousie Community Mennonite Brethren Church in Calgary.

 **Eleanor M. Loewen** is assistant professor at Catherine Booth Bible College in Winnipeg. She comes to this position by way of recent congregational responsibilities in two United churches in Winnipeg, as education consultant for the Conference of Mennonites in Canada, as Director of Student Services for the General Conference Mennonite Church, as well as positions at Bethel, Bluffton, and Goshen colleges.

She was born in Calgary, Alberta, but calls Abbotsford, British Columbia, home. She obtained her education primarily by "Mennoniting" her way through high school, Canadian Mennonite Bible College, Goshen College, and Mennonite Biblical Seminary. Indiana University was the site for M.S. Ed. and Ed.D. degree work.

She makes frequent trips to be with immediate and extended families in British Columbia. An "adopted" member of her family is Ramok Toshi Imchen, whom she sponsored as a music student at Canadian Mennonite Bible College and Goshen College.

Congregational involvements include being chairperson of the Charleswood Mennonite Church worship and pastoral care commission and member of the church council. She also participates in worship leading and preaching.